REGRET

REGRET

A THEOLOGY

PAUL J. GRIFFITHS

University of Notre Dame Press
Notre Dame, Indiana

Published by the University of Notre Dame Press

Library of Congress Control Number: 2020950580

ISBN: 978-0-268-20025-1 (Hardback)
ISBN: 978-0-268-20026-8 (Paperback)
ISBN: 978-0-268-20024-4 (WebPDF)
ISBN: 978-0-268-20027-5 (Epub)

this book is for the regretful

The past may or may not be a foreign country. It may morph or lie still, but its capital is always Regret.

—ANDRÉ ACIMAN

What she [Anna Karenina] did she now finds insupportable, because she could have been justified only by the life she hoped for, and those hopes were not just negated, but refuted, by what happened. . . . [T]he constitutive thought of regret in general is something like "how much better if it had been otherwise."

—BERNARD WILLIAMS

Herein lies the rub of the antithetical thread: envisaging how other choices might have constructed the life you've actually lived. Years could atrophy in the ciphering of it.

—EIMEAR MCBRIDE

CONTENTS

PREFACE

IN THIS BOOK I OFFER A SPECULATIVE THEOLOGICAL DEPICTION of what it means to wish things otherwise, and of how best to engage in that complicated activity. I write as a Catholic theologian who has in mind the deliverances of the teaching Church on the matters I write about; sometimes those deliverances surface, more often they don't, but they remain a constant informing presence. I intend, principally, clarification and speculative extension of the grammar of Christian thought and talk about regret, remorse, contrition, and associated topics. That purpose entails the unlikelihood that all the positions I entertain and defend in this book are true. But since one of the theologian's tasks is to sketch patterns of thought and argument that grow from orthodox Christianity but are not (yet) part of it, that isn't a problem. Theology should be, first and last, about and responsive to the triune LORD who is its principal topic; it should then seek to be interesting; it is no part of the Catholic theologian's remit to be right.

I build here upon theological positions taken in earlier works, specifically *Intellectual Appetite* (2009), my commentary on the Song of Songs (2011), my eschatological treatise *Decreation* (2014), and *Christian Flesh* (2018). I've learned a good deal from criticisms of those works, and I have modified some of the positions entertained in them and dropped others. But in many cases, the positions offered in this book have roots in and presuppose sketches and arguments given in more detail in those earlier works, and for this reason I here refer readers to them. A few phrases and sentences from one or another of those works appear in this one.

The method adopted here is direct and simple. It's grammatical: I attempt to write what can be written about wishing things otherwise using the lexicon and syntax provided me by a particular construal of the Christian-theological archive, which is to say the library of texts significant for the Christian tradition. There are a few arguments in the book, but mostly it's a depiction of what might reasonably, if speculatively, be taken as well-formed utterances of a Christian sort about regret and its kin — and, concomitantly, a depiction and rejection of ill-formed utterances about them. Apart from engagement with some passages of scripture, I largely eschew explicit engagement with texts from the Christian archive to pursue these purposes. That's not because I'm indifferent to such texts or think there's nothing to be learned from them. Quite the reverse. Much of what I've written here is stimulated by what I've read from that archive, and there are, as the knowledgeable reader will easily see, many echoes of, disagreements with, and affirmations of what's to be found there. I choose not to quote or engage in exegesis mostly because the lines of a sketch are easily obscured by doing that, and what I hope for is a clear line.

In addition to scripture, I often quote and discuss works of fiction and poetry that have to do in one way or another with wishing things otherwise. Some of these works are by Christians, some by pagans, and some by Jews. I treat them as artifacts of Christian-theological interest because theological thought can be provoked by works that show something, lapidarily and gnomically, just as well as by those that expound or argue. Poetical and fictional depictions of regret very often do a better job of such provocation than do analyses in theological treatises.

Some conventions to note: LORD, uppercased, represents the divine name. When I use "god," I lowercase it, initial and all, unless I'm quoting someone else who doesn't. The reasons for this are provided in my *Decreation*. I quote and elaborate upon scripture always and only in the Latin of the *Nova Vulgata*; all translations from that text are my own. The justification for this is given in my "Which Are the Words of Scripture?" (*Theological Studies*, 2011). Lastly, about pronouns. "We" means one of three things: you and me, reader, the two of us working together; or, we Christians—you may not be one, and if you're not you can eavesdrop; or, we human beings. "You" picks out the one reading these words now. "I" indicates the one writing these words now. I don't use pronouns for the LORD, but I do for Jesus, gendered masculine. Eschewing pronouns for the LORD, and writing the divine name thus, leads, when the LORD is being discussed, to a costive and clotted English prose. That's good. It makes clear that writing and reading about the LORD doesn't come easily. Language and thought go on holiday when they attempt that task, and their vacancy is evident.

ACKNOWLEDGMENTS

I'M GRATEFUL TO THOSE WHO'VE HELPED ME TO THINK THROUGH the matters treated in this book by way of face-to-face and epistolary conversation. Most important here are Brendan Case, Del Kiernan-Lewis, Philip Porter, and Lauren Winner. An important initial stimulus was provided by Sheryl Overmyer, who has herself been thinking about some of these matters for a good while, and who was kind enough to provide me with her working bibliography on regret and associated questions; she was also, supererogatorily, kind enough to read an early draft of the whole and to provide comments and questions that have significantly affected this final version. I'm also grateful to those, living and dead, who've helped me by writing on these topics. I couldn't have written this book without their work. The more important among them are listed in the bibliography at the back of this volume.

I also acknowledge publishers who've been gracious enough to grant permission to quote copyrighted material: For Paul Celan, excerpts from "Mapesbury Road," translated by Michael Hamburger, from *Poems of Paul Celan*. Translation copyright © 1972, 1980, 1988, 1995 by Michael Hamburger. Reprinted with the permission of the publishers, Persea Books, Inc (New York), www.perseabooks.com. All rights reserved. For Emily Dickinson's "Remorse," as it appears in *The Poems of Emily Dickinson: Reading Edition*, edited by Ralph W. Franklin, Cambridge, MA: The Belknap Press of Harvard University Press, copyright © 1998, 1999 by the President and Fellows of

CHAPTER ONE

The LORD's Regrets

CHRISTIANS WRITING THEOLOGY SHOULD BEGIN BY WRITING about the LORD. It's therefore appropriate to begin a study of the otherwise-attitudes—that is, the attitudes that have what's expressed by the sentence "I would it were otherwise" at their heart—by writing about the oddity that the LORD, like us it seems, exhibits those attitudes. The LORD, too, is shown in scripture to wish otherwise things that have happened, including states of affairs the LORD has brought about, and to act upon those wishes. How is this to be interpreted?

It's something close to dogma for Catholic Christians that the LORD is timeless, in the strict sense that no temporal properties are the LORD's. This is one entailment of understanding the LORD as simple, which is to say thinking that there is, in the LORD, no distinction between essence and accident, between what the LORD is and what the LORD has. The LORD's wisdom is what the LORD is, the LORD's love is what the LORD is, the LORD's gift is what the LORD is, and so on for all putative divine properties. From such a view it follows that the LORD can have no properties at one time that the LORD lacks at another: everything that the LORD is (which is simply being the LORD, the one who is, which is what the LORD says to Moses in the third chapter of Exodus when asked for a name: *ego sum qui sum*), the LORD is atemporally. This is difficult doctrine, and controversial; it presses particularly hard upon the otherwise-attitudes, for those seem to entail not only that those who have them are located in time but also that they can judge that something done didn't work out, wasn't the best thing to do, and ought, if possible, to be redressed. It's not at once obvious how properties such as these can be predicated of the LORD.

IN THE LATIN VERSIONS OF SCRIPTURE (THE CLEMENTINE VULGATE and the New Vulgate are the same in this respect), the LORD whom Christians confess is often represented with directness and clarity as wishing things otherwise, which is the fundamental otherwise-thought, and then as acting upon that thought. The standard vocabulary is *paenitentia* (noun), and *paenitere* (verb), predicated of the LORD. How to render this in English isn't obvious. You might try saying that the LORD is penitent or cultivates penitence, but that doesn't seem quite right, given the more-or-less technical sense given to penitence (and penance) in Catholic theology and as a result, to some degree, in secular English. Scripture doesn't suggest that the LORD has sinned and must now acknowledge that sin, and do whatever can be done to redress it. Rather, *paenitentia* is closer to regret, to wishing otherwise something that is, regrettably, the case. Regret, then, shading into repentance: wishing some state of affairs otherwise, and turning away from—repenting—the LORD's own part in making it so.

The standard schema is that the LORD sees that something hasn't worked out as well as it might have, as a result of human sin or misprision or some other mistake; then the LORD regrets, laments, and is angry that this unsatisfactoriness obtains and does something to prevent it continuing, typically by making a judgment and either acting or threatening to act upon that judgment; then the LORD, regretting the judgment (in response to some turn of events—human pleas, human contrition, human repentance, and so on), rescinds it or in some other fashion turns away from it.

A good instance is the story of Saul and the Amalekites in the fifteenth chapter of the first book of Samuel. The LORD commands Saul to fight the Amalekites and to slaughter them all, along with every animal they own. Saul fights, as commanded, but he doesn't kill Agag, king of the Amalekites, and he likewise spares the lives of some among the animals, for what seem to be good-enough reasons, including the intention to sacrifice the best among the Amalekites' livestock to the LORD. The LORD, seeing this, says to Samuel: "I regret-repent having made Saul king (*paenitet me quod constituerim Saul regem*) because he has abandoned me and hasn't done what I said (*quia derelequit me et verba mea opere non implevit*)" — words repeated verbatim later in the chapter. Here it's clear that the LORD is regretting something the LORD has done — making Saul king — as well as Saul's particular disobedience. What's regrettable, and regretted, isn't just a state of affairs traceable without remainder to human agency, but also the LORD's establishment of conditions that made particular sins possible. Saul couldn't have disobeyed in the way that he did without being king, and so the LORD regrets not only Saul's sin but also the LORD's own act in making Saul king.

But, a little later in the same chapter, Samuel, when telling Saul of the LORD's judgment, says:

> The LORD has today ripped rule over Israel away from you and given it to one close to you who is better than you [that is, David]. Furthermore, the Glory of Israel doesn't lie and isn't moved by regret-repentance, for he isn't human so that he might regret-repent. (1 Samuel 15:28–29)

In chapter 15, then, *paenitentia* is both affirmed and denied of the LORD: the LORD both does and doesn't do this. And it's not just that the LORD is said to regret one thing but not another thing. No, it's a more direct contradiction than that: the LORD says to Samuel that what's in play is the LORD's regret at or repentance for having made Saul king; and Samuel says to Saul that the LORD isn't one who has regret-repentance at all, and the LORD can't have regret-repentance because those are human attitudes, not possible for the LORD. It's clear in context that what Samuel says the LORD doesn't regret is having taken the kingship from Saul, which is compatible with regretting having made Saul king in the first place. But the strength of Samuel's formulation goes far beyond what would have made that smaller point. Saul's response to all this is to acknowledge that he has sinned in not following the LORD's instructions to the letter, and to offer worship to the LORD. Samuel's response is to have the trembling Agag brought before him and then to kill him by cutting him in pieces. In that way, what Saul should have done is brought about.

This story is the clearest juxtaposition in scripture of the affirmation that the LORD does repent-regret with the affirmation that the LORD does no such thing, and moreover that the LORD doesn't do that thing because of who the LORD is—neither human nor creature. I resolve the difficulty below and rejoice, as any interpreter of scripture should, to find such a clear case of prima facie contradiction; such instances are efficacious in prompting theological thought because of the axiom that the canon of scripture is not incoherent. The only thing to say for now is that the presence of the tension here shows clearly that worries about the propriety of saying that the LORD regrets-repents are themselves scriptural, even while scripture again and again says just that of the LORD.

A second instance of the LORD's regret-repentance occurs in the sixth chapter of Genesis. It's written that the sons of god, seeing that human women are beautiful, have sex with them, and children are born of these acts of intercourse. Among the LORD's responses to this sin (one, presumably, of miscegenation), is:

> seeing that human wickedness was multiplying on earth, and that all human thoughts were always intent only on evil, the LORD regret-repented that he'd made humans on earth, and grieved inwardly, and said: "I'll delete the human beings I've created from the face of the earth—from humans to beasts to reptiles to the birds of the air—for I regret-repent having made them." (Genesis 6:5–7)

The twice-affirmed regret is a deep one. The LORD regret-repents having created humans at all, and does so because of their sins. The LORD's response to this regret is to delete not only human creatures but all others from the earth, with the exception of Noah, his family, and the creatures that can fit into the Ark. The pattern is like the one evident in Saul's case: the LORD does something new (makes Saul king / creates human beings); the new state of affairs the LORD has brought about gets damaged by the actions of the creatures in it; the LORD judges this, makes the content of the judgment explicit, and undoes an element of the damaged pattern (deposes Saul / deletes all human beings except Noah and his family). There's a further similarity: the LORD's regret-based action is laced with mercy, evident in the fact that flowing from it are goods that otherwise wouldn't have been (David's kingship / the renewal of the cosmos after the flood).

A third instance, and this a peculiarly clear one, is in the book of Jonah. Jonah is instructed by the LORD to preach judgment to the people of Nineveh because of their sins. "Only forty days and Nineveh will be laid waste," he says to the Ninevites, reluctantly—he's spent a good deal of effort trying to avoid this duty, and the text is clear that he has no desire to do it. When they hear Jonah, the people of Nineveh, from the king downward, believe what the LORD is saying to them through Jonah; they fast and cover themselves with sackcloth, saying, "Who knows? God might turn away (*convertere*) and forgive; he might turn back (*revertere*) from his fierce anger so that we won't perish." As a result, "God saw what they did, how they turned away (*convertere*) from their evil ways, and god had mercy on that evil and didn't do what he'd said he would do" (Jonah 3:1–10).

Here's another instance, it seems, of the LORD's regret-repentance, although signalled with a different vocabulary. The language of the third chapter of Jonah turns around the verb *vertere* (to turn, to change, to reverse) combined with two different prefixes, *re-* and *con-*. The English calques for these, "revert" and "convert," unfortunately won't do as renderings; they've accumulated too many other meanings in English, some of them in almost direct contradiction to what's being said in Jonah. The renderings "turn back," for *revertere*, and "turn away," for *convertere*, aren't transparent to the Latin, but they do keep the "turn" element of the root verb and do capture what seems to be the near-synonymy of these verbs in the text. The lexical and conceptual point, in any case, is that what the people of Nineveh do in turning away from their sins is the same as what the LORD does in turning away from judgment: the same verb is used for both. In each case, a change is indicated from one course or kind of action to another, in opposition to the first one. And in each case, the change is prompted by a particular event: in one case it is prompted by Jonah's preaching and in the other by the Ninevites' fasting. Each is alike in structure and alike, therefore, in being a case of regret-repentance, here understood as (something like) a decision that a previous course of action is no longer appropriate and needs to be otherwised in intention and, so far as possible, also in action.

Jonah isn't happy about the LORD's regret-repentance. He says in the fourth chapter: "O LORD . . . I knew [when you first called me to preach to the Ninevites] that you are a gracious and merciful god, long-suffering and rich in mercy, forgiving of evil" (Jonah 4:2). The thought is that Jonah knew from the beginning that the LORD would be unlikely to follow through on the threat of judgment and that he's now been shown to be right about that. The LORD's response to this complaint is to make a shrub grow up to give shade to Jonah, now outside the city, and then, in short order, to destroy the same shrub. Jonah is angry that his shade has been destroyed, and the LORD, arguing from the lesser to the greater case, says that if Jonah is right to care about the fate of a shrub, shouldn't the LORD be right to care about the fate of a city? This response doesn't at all address the difficulty about the LORD's regret-repentance; it rather underlines merciful rescinding of judgment as a nonnegotiable fact about, or feature of, the LORD as the LORD seems to us.

A final instance of the LORD's regret-repentance is in the eighteenth chapter of Jeremiah. The prophet is sent to a potter's house, where he sees the potter remaking a failed, misshapen vessel. The LORD speaks to him:

Look [house of Israel], you're in my hands as clay is in the potter's. I might speak at any moment against a people or a kingdom, saying that I will eradicate, destroy, and disperse it; if that people regret-repents its evil because of what I've said against it, I too will regret-repent the evil I'd thought to do to it. Also, I might suddenly say of a people or kingdom that I will build it up and plant it; but if it should do what looks evil to me, so that it doesn't hear my voice, I'll regret-repent the good I said I'd do for it. (Jeremiah 18:6–10)

The broadside scattering of subjunctives of various strengths in this passage is remarkable. It's a feature of otherwise-thinking in general that it's counterfactual and occurs largely in subjunctive or optative moods (Latin doesn't mark a distinction between these), and in this passage regret and longing are interlaced—regret, that is, for a people addressed by but not listening to the LORD, and longing for a people that will listen. The passage is also a clear statement of the general principle: the LORD's *paenitentia* can turn the LORD from judgment to mercy, or from mercy to judgment; and in either case, the turn occurs because of what we do or don't do. There is inextricable intimacy between the LORD's repentance and ours; the former is never discussed without the latter, and for the LORD to regret-repent it is certainly necessary, and perhaps sufficient, that something changes. The LORD's regret-repentance is always responsive and always, in the end, transfigurative. These are features of the LORD's action as it appears from within the order of time, from the perspective, that is, of time's passage.

A more expansive version of the scriptural pattern on this matter can be seen by looking at Jesus. It isn't that Jesus is himself ever clearly depicted in the New Testament as performing regret in the way that the LORD is shown to do in the Old. Jesus laments, certainly, over Jerusalem and over Lazarus and over the hard-heartedness of those he speaks to. But he's never shown to decide on a course of action, begin implementing it, and then, on seeing that something has changed, reverse course and do something different. He can be persuaded, sometimes, to do something that at first he wasn't intending to do—by the Syro-Phoenician woman, for instance; or by the woman at the well; or, perhaps, by the centurion. But even that isn't quite the same as the pattern apparent in the stories about Saul or Jonah. In those, there's a settled course of action already undertaken by the LORD and then a reversal of course that involves acknowledgment that what had been undertaken was a mistake, or at least hadn't yielded the fruit it was intended and thought likely to yield. This pattern isn't clearly evident in any particular action of Jesus. But it is evident, at least arguably so, in the large event of Jesus, which is to say the incarnation, crucifixion, resurrection, and ascension.

Jesus's incarnation is a settled course of action on the LORD's part—decided, undertaken, and full of beauty and goodness. In all these things it is like the LORD's creation of humans. The incarnation, however, leads to the crucifixion and the tomb, to the destruction and absence that is remembered and redone on (Good) Friday. Similarly, the presence of human creatures on the earth devastates it, and this leads to their deletion from it, as in the sixth chapter of Genesis. Destruction and absence again. The crucifixion is followed, on Sunday, by resurrection, which is the renewed and transfigured presence of Jesus in the world in the flesh as preparation for the sacrament of salvation that is his body, the Church. Similarly, the deletion of human creatures from the earth is followed, after the dove has returned to the Ark, by humans' renewed presence on a renewed earth in the ambiguously sacramental presence of Noah, with whom a covenant binding the LORD to the whole human race is made—and from which covenant, just around the corner in the order of time, is the call of Abraham and the unambiguous establishment of the Jewish people as the sacrament of salvation.

The language of regret and repentance isn't used in the story of Jesus. But the story has the same structure as those that do use that language. The LORD does something, and then undoes it, and then redoes it, transfiguratively, so that the outcome is better than it would have been had the undoing not intervened—David is an improvement on Saul, the post-flood world an improvement on the pre-flood devastation, and the risen and ascended flesh of Jesus an improvement, blasphemous though it sounds to say so, on his natal flesh. (The principal "improvements" come in the non-restriction of the risen and ascended flesh to map-gridded space and clock-ticked time.) Regretful repentance occurs on the LORD's part at the stage of undoing: something, some state of affairs, must be undone in order for some damage to be redressed, and the undoing involves, or may rightly be said to involve, penitent regret on the LORD's part. This involvement can most clearly be seen in the New Testament's Jesus-narrative at the moment of Jesus's agony at Gethsemane. The undoing is upon him, and he wants it about as much as the LORD wants to delete humanity from the world. Luke's Gospel, in its twenty-second chapter, has it that Jesus's sweat, as he prays in the garden that he might not suffer and die on the cross, is *sicut guttae sanguinis decurrentis in terram*—like blood-drops raining upon the earth. So also for the LORD's *paenitentia* at the great deletion of the flood.

THE PATTERN IS CLEAR. IN THE CASE—THE PARADIGMATIC CASE— of the crucifixion and resurrection, though, it sounds odd, perhaps artificial, to use the language of regret or repentance. That's not only because the language is absent from scripture. It's also because the LORD's atemporal mode of being is closer to the surface of the New Testament accounts of Jesus than it is in the story of Jonah or that of Noah. The Jonah story depends for its narrative force on a depiction of the LORD's responsiveness to what the Ninevites do, absent any suggestion that this was foreknown or preordained. Jonah isn't surprised by the LORD's turning away from the condemnation of the Ninevites, but not because he thinks the LORD knows what will happen; rather, it's because he understands it to be an ordinary pattern that the LORD responds mercifully to even the suggestion of repentance on our part, and he expects this to happen in the case of Nineveh too. The language of regret and repentance sits more comfortably, rhetorically and conceptually, in narratives whose tension requires that their outcomes not be known and shown in advance. Neither the Jonah nor the Saul story would work as narratives if all parties were shown to know at all points how things would go. The LORD's repentance belongs, narratively speaking, to contexts in which the LORD's involvement with the temporal order is emphasized, and it is a central need of both Jews and Christians to do that: the LORD, for both, is an agent responsive to temporal needs and events, and must, sometimes, be depicted as such.

But for Christians at least, and I expect for Jews also, there are other registers for thought and speech and writing. We need to depict the LORD theoretically as well; thinking and writing about the LORD as an agent in history and time with desires and disappointments and regrets and (even) contrition serves our need to understand the LORD as LORD of history, one whose sovereignty includes and is implicated in everything of importance to us, and those needs are widespread and of fundamental importance to Christians. There are few, if any, Christians who lack a sense of the LORD as responsive to immediate need. Even when that sense is lacking, it's generally understood to be desirable and its lack something to be remedied, if possible. Thinking of the LORD as regretful and repentant and contrite belongs in the context of thinking about the LORD as responsive to immediate need, and there is nothing problematic about it. But some Christians, as well as some who aren't, need also to think of and about the LORD in such a way as to discriminate the LORD from everything that is not the LORD—which is to say, from the created order. Thinking in that way requires different things to be said. Among these things is the claim that the LORD is atemporal and simple, which is one way of saying what must be said if the LORD is not, in the theoretical register, to be assimilated to and included among creatures. The LORD doesn't share a mode of being with creatures exactly because they are creatures and the LORD is creator, and creator, moreover, out of nothing—neither out of the LORDself, nor out of something (what would it be?) existing independently of the LORD. The LORD gives being as sheer noncontractual gift, and so there is no univocal predication of being: to say "the LORD exists" and "you exist" is not to predicate identically of you and the LORD. Were it so, the upshot would be that you and the LORD would exist in the same way, the LORD would, like you, have been created *ex nihilo*, and the LORD would therefore not be the LORD. That is a reduction to absurdity.

The register in which the language of the immediately preceding sentences moves is different from that to which the passages from Jonah, Jeremiah, Genesis, and the first book of Samuel belong. The differences are given by different needs and purposes in something like the same way that endearments are differentiated from police-report descriptions. I may say to my beloved, and even to others, that she is the most beautiful woman in the world and the only woman for me; in describing her to the police I may say that she is of such-and-such a height and weight and age, with hair of this color and eyes of that. It isn't the case that what I say to the police and what I say to her are in contradiction; neither is it the case that one set of claims is true and the other false; neither is it the case that there's any place or perspective from which you might reasonably say of one or another kind of talk, "that's the real thing—that's the right way to talk about her." There are many ways to talk about beloveds, and their differences are given by context and need and purpose, and not according to some context-free scale of values (there are none of those). It would be a mistake, certainly, to substitute the language of the bedroom for that of the police report, or vice-versa. Similarly for theoretical and narratival-devotional talk about the LORD. It isn't that the LORD is really atemporal and simple and has regrets only by courtesy. Neither is it the case that the LORD really has regrets and is said to be atemporal and simple and so on only by courtesy. Rather, it's the case that Christian grammar requires both things to be said, though in different contexts and for different purposes. It's also the case that Christian grammar eschews the thought that there's a single register that satisfactorily comprises everything that needs to be said about the LORD. Christian grammar is in this an instance of a general truth about human thought and talk.

Not all Christians agree about this. Those with theoretical proclivities are likely to think they've understood the LORD rightly in seeing that the otherwise-attitudes cannot be predicated of the LORD on pain of making the LORD a creature. And those clear about the responsiveness of the LORD to events in time are likely to think that the LORD really is so responsive. The problem lies with the adverbs "really" and "rightly." Scripture and tradition require that the otherwise-attitudes be affirmed of the LORD in some contexts and for some purposes, and denied in others. They do not require the further claim that the affirmation is rightly made and the denial wrongly—or vice-versa. Thinking that one saying is rightly said and

the other wrongly involves the importation and deployment of philosophical methods and convictions that have no place in Christianity's
grammar and that are otherwise problematic.

The LORD, then, not being human, is exempt from regret and
repentance. And the LORD regret-repents, among other things,
having made Saul king in Israel, and acts to undo that prior act. Both
these things are said, if you recall, in the fifteenth chapter of the first
book of Samuel. Both need to be said. Similarly, my beloved is the
most beautiful of women. And my beloved cannot be discriminated
from other women by appeal to her beauty. Different registers are in
play for each saying. On the one hand, the Saul story emphasizes the
intimate engagement of the LORD with the events of Saul's and
Samuel's and Israel's life; in that register, of course, the LORD has
regrets and repentances and hopes and fears and anticipations. The
LORD is, in that register, feared and implored and eagerly examined
for readable signs of what's next. And on the other hand, the story
sometimes, as in this case, warns those who speak to and of the LORD
in that first register that there are dangers in doing so, dangers intensified when that's the only register used. Among them is the danger
that the LORD can begin to appear as one more player on the stage
of gods and men, one who is like us except a bit more powerful, one
who is, therefore, of only local, here-and-now, significance. One way
of performing the warning is to do what Samuel does, which is shifting
registers by reminding Saul that as well as the LORD being the one
who regrets having made him king, the LORD is the one who is
altogether outside the sphere of regret. A parallel warning in the reverse direction, not found clearly in scripture although broadly implied in it, would be to interrupt a remorseless focus on theological
technicality—on, say, the difficulties of construing the relations between divine and human action on the understanding that the LORD
is simple—with a laconic but direct mention of the LORD's election
of Abraham or Jesus's sadness at the death of Lazarus. Those im-
mersed in theology in this technical sense are likely to forget the
LORD's intimate, temporally indexed concern with Israel's and the
Church's and their own life, and to become correspondingly uneasy
with the register in which those truths are explicit. This is at least as

damaging a mistake as coming to think of the LORD as a creature. Those whose theology erases the temporal-devotional register, or relativizes it as lower-order talk, good enough for those who don't know better, will find that their love for the LORD lasts about as long as an endearment-free marriage.

So the first book of Samuel doesn't contradict itself any more than I would were I to say in the bedroom that my beloved is the most beautiful of women and then to say in the police report that she's an ordinary-looking woman of forty or so. The tension between the two claims in 1 Samuel 15—which may be put in brief as *the LORD regrets Saul* and *the LORD has no regrets*—isn't to be resolved by adding the modifier "really" to one or other of the claims. That would create a hierarchy by taking one of the claims to be true and the other to be merely rhetorical, and then requiring the latter to be interpreted in terms of and via the constraints of the former. It's to be resolved, rather, by affirming both, seeing what part each plays in the discourse-register to which it belongs, and guarding against the transferral (to another register) of claims belonging to one register. Bedroom-language can't easily be transferred to the police report, or the other way around; but that isn't because the claims belonging to the one are more true or more accurate than those belonging to the other.

For Christians, the liturgy can help here. It often juxtaposes, startlingly and without any attempt at resolution, language from a technical-theological register with language from a temporal-historical register. The Niceno-Constantinopolitan confession, for instance, contains technical-theoretical sonorities in the trinitarian and christo-logical spheres (*consubstantialem*), followed almost at once by blunt historical-temporal particularities (*crucifixus etiam pro nobis sub Pontio Pilato*). No third register, apart from the context of the liturgy as a whole, is provided to reconcile and embrace the two, and neither is one elevated hierarchically above the other. The truth is given, rather, exactly by their co-occurrence without hierarchical resolution. It's the same with the Saul story: the LORD regrets Saul, and the LORD, not being human, regrets nothing. That's what Christians say, and when pressed for a rule of discourse that adjudicates the tension by removing one side of it, they (we) firmly say that there's no such rule and that the expectation of one is a feature of pagan, not Christian, thought. Christians, when they are fluent, know when to say what; pagans, by listening attentively, can learn how it goes.

IT'S AN AXIOM OF CHRISTIAN THOUGHT THAT HUMAN LIVES participate in the LORD's life with greater intimacy than do other kinds of lives—plant lives, or non-human-animal lives, for example. That's because we are *imago dei*, the very image of the LORD, in ways that other creatures are not, and because the LORD's enfleshment was as one of us and not as some other creature. (There are difficulties here, not least about the extension of "us": Is it the same as that of the species *Homo sapiens*? And what's the extension of that species? But those are not difficulties to be resolved here.) Among the implications of that intimacy is that coming to understand something of the pattern of the LORD's life is suggestive for understanding the pattern of our own. This can be put as a procedural principle of theological thinking: theological anthropology is best done by thinking first about the LORD. This is as true of the otherwise-attitudes as it is with respect to other topics in theological anthropology. And so it's good at this point to recapitulate what's been learned about the LORD's otherwise-passions. The pattern is as follows: the LORD does something; the state of affairs the LORD has brought about gets damaged; the LORD makes explicit what's gone wrong; and the LORD acts to redress the damage, bringing into being in so doing felicities that would not otherwise have occurred. (Job's children die horribly, by the LORD's permission—but the LORD makes this good by providing him new and better ones, as is strikingly and horribly implied at the end of the book.) And, at the same time, the LORD is neither subject to nor altered by time's passage. Our otherwise-attitudes participate in this pattern and are, therefore, patterned by it.

One aspect of this pattern deserves emphasis, in part because of the difficulty in seeing how our otherwise-attitudes can be patterned by it. The LORD's regrets entail turning away from a failed or damaged experiment and beginning a fresh one. Because it's the LORD doing this new thing, whatever it is (David's kingship, the floodwaters receding from a renewed earth, the resurrection), the new thing is a felicity, or at least involves felicities. Not only that, the felicities wouldn't have come to be had there not been the damage of the first failure. Suppose this to be the case. Suppose the LORD's otherwise-attitudes and the actions that flow from them always and necessarily transfigure that damage so that things are better than they would have been had the damage not occurred in the first place—or, if it's too difficult to make judgments of that kind, at least that the LORD's regret-motivated actions always bring particular goods to be that otherwise wouldn't have been (Job's improved children). Is regret or remorse or contrition appropriate if it's clear already (it always is to the LORD) that the putatively regrettable state of affairs carries felicities with it, in its wake, at least? At first blush, the answer is that any damage is regrettable even if its occurrence is a necessary condition for the emergence of some good or goods. It's perfectly proper to regret the pains of childbirth even when the outcome is a healthy child. Regrets of that kind were among the motivators for the development of effective anaesthesia. That you now have better vision in your left eye than you had before its retina detached doesn't mean that the pain of the detachment isn't to be mourned and wished otherwise— as is the fact that our bodies are subject to that kind of trauma. There are complications here, however, and they can be clarified within the grammar of Christian thought by addressing the idea that culpable faults, *culpae*, can be, and perhaps always are, felicitous or at least bring felicities with them.

CHAPTER TWO

Faults

IT'S A COMMONPLACE OF CHRISTIAN THEOLOGY THAT THERE are felicitous faults, *culpae*, that bring *felices* with them. Eve and Adam's eating of the forbidden fruit in the garden is the obvious and standard example. This commonplace raises questions about the otherwise-attitudes. If a fault brings felicities with it, as (perhaps) the Fall brought Jesus, ought it to be wished otherwise? Might not a fault's felicities, in an extreme case, mean that it would be a mistake to regret it, a mistake, even, to understand it as a fault? Perhaps it's the case that all faults bring felicities with them, even felicities that outweigh the faults. If that's so, might the category of fault itself need to be abandoned? If everything shall be well, what is there to wish otherwise? Saul brings David; without Saul, no David; why then regret Saul, why wish his faults otherwise if he, with his faults, is necessary for David and, therefore, for Jesus?

THE COMMONPLACE IS MOST CLEARLY EVIDENT IN THE characterization of the disobedience of Eve and Adam in the garden—their rebellious eating of the forbidden fruit—as a *felix culpa*, a fault or transgression that is also fruitful, productive of goods for which it is at least a necessary condition. There is ground for this understanding in scripture. The serpent, replying to Eve's claim that she has been forbidden by the LORD on pain of death to touch or eat the fruit of the tree of the knowledge of good and evil at the heart of paradise, says, in the third chapter of Genesis: "No, you won't die the death [if you eat that fruit], for god knows that in whatever day you eat it your eyes will be opened and you will be like god, knowing good and evil" (Genesis 3:4–5). The serpent doesn't lie. As Genesis goes on to show, when they eat the forbidden fruit, their eyes are opened and they understand matters they hadn't understood before. Those matters include their own nakedness and disobedience, which make them shamefaced before one another and fearful of the LORD's anger. Knowledge of good and evil, which is what the forbidden fruit gives to those who eat it, can be read as the capacity to make moral distinctions and thereby to know when one has not done what one ought, or has done what one ought not. Without the eating, no moral capacity. The judgments on Adam and Eve's part that their nakedness needs to be hidden, and that the LORD needs to be hidden from, are evidence of the making of just such distinctions: nakedness has become morally problematic, and the LORD has become one to be feared and hidden from because wrong has been done.

The serpent's prediction is shown, in this respect at least, to be accurate. This doesn't by itself show that the capacity to make moral distinctions is itself felicitous, and it therefore doesn't at once support a view of the Fall as a felicitous fault. Genesis, after all, ends its third chapter like this:

> The LORD god expelled him [Adam, with Eve] from the paradise of Eden so that he might work the soil from which he had been taken. He drove the man out, and he placed cherubim at the east of the paradise of Eden, and a flaming sword whirling to guard the way to the tree of life. (Genesis 3:23–24)

That punishment, together with preceding curses on the serpent, Eve, and Adam, doesn't suggest much by way of felicitousness. And yet, the LORD also says:

> Behold the man who has become like one of us in knowing good and evil. Now, therefore, he might reach out his hand and take and eat from the tree of life and live forever. (Genesis 3:22)

That is a full endorsement of what the serpent earlier said to Eve. Eating the forbidden fruit makes those who eat it in some respects *quasi unus ex nobis,* "like one of us"—which is to say, like one of us gods. The back-and-forth between singular and plural in these texts is remarkable: the serpent promises Eve that she'll be "like god" (*sicut Deus,* singular) if she eats; but when the LORD speaks the assimilation becomes plural, which suggests to the Christian reader the persons of the Trinity—to be like the LORD is to be like the triune LORD, Father, Son, and Spirit—and, to the attentive reader of scripture, the many-membered class of gods over which the LORD rules as king over the other gods, as, among many other places, in the opening verses of Psalm 95. The assimilation of Eve and Adam to the LORD is evident in their capacity to discriminate good from evil, which makes that capacity unambiguously felicitous. The further acknowledgment by the LORD that those who can discriminate good from evil might, should they eat from the tree of life, also become immortal suggests that eating the forbidden fruit is also felicitous in another respect: it might, if coupled with or followed by eating the fruit of the tree of life, which wasn't at first forbidden, yield eternal life, and the LORD banishes Eve and Adam from Eden and guards the way back so that the felicity of eternal life, whose possibility is an effect of the Fall, might be denied to human creatures.

The sequence of threats and promises about death in the opening chapters of Genesis is capable of many readings. There are two trees at Eden's heart, the tree of life and the tree of knowledge. The second tree's fruit is forbidden, with the promise-threat from the LORD that those who eat it will "die the death" (*morte morieris*), an apparently pleonastic phrase that could also be rendered "die with death." Eve, in recounting this promise-threat to the serpent, elides the pleonasm and says only that the LORD commanded her and Adam not to eat so that they might not die (*ne moriamur*). The serpent's reply retrieves the pleonasm and assures Eve that those who eat the forbidden fruit won't die the death (die with death). The LORD then says to Adam: "In the sweat of your brow you'll eat bread until you return from the soil from which you were taken—because you are dust, and to dust you will return" (Genesis 3:19). The curse is secured by barring the way back to the tree of life.

If the pleonasm *morte moriari* ("die the death") is ignored, the sequence is clear enough. All parties agree that the command to abstain from the forbidden fruit comes with the threat of death. The serpent claims that the threat is empty, and that instead the result of eating will be assimilation to the LORD. Once the fruit is eaten, the LORD agrees that what the serpent has said is correct, specifies that such assimilation would include immortality if the fruit of the tree of life were eaten, and takes action to make that impossible while at the same time condemning Adam, and by implication Eve, to an eventual ordinary death—a return to dust.

But what about the pleonasm? It's axiomatic for Christians that the text of scripture has no accidental features, which entails that the pleonasm isn't one. And it's by way of the pleonasm that the LORD promises and the serpent denies. Clearly, Eve and Adam do not at once die as a result of eating the forbidden fruit: if that's what *morte moriari* means, then the serpent, once again, is right. But it's preferable, or at least possible, to read *morte moriari* not to indicate death but rather to indicate the condition of mortality. On this reading, the death that is the instrument of our dying is the fact of our mortality. That's what kills us. It's not that eating the forbidden fruit brings death, simpliciter and at once; rather, it brings mortality (*mortalitas*) by means of which Eve and Adam will eventually die. If the text is read like this, then the serpent is wrong. Human creatures are, after the Fall, mortal, even if this condition has to be carefully guarded against its remedy, which is eating from the tree of life.

It's possible, then, to see at least one felicity in the Fall, culpable though it was. The felicity is that the Fall opens a way to a condition otherwise unattainable: that of life like the LORD's life—of, in short, divinization, which doesn't mean becoming the LORD but rather becoming as like (recall that *quasi*) the LORD as is possible for human creatures, a likeness that includes life without end accompanied by an understanding of the goodness of that life. For Catholics, it's doctrine that death is not a natural condition and that Eve and Adam would not have died without the Fall. But the life without end they would have had if they hadn't fallen would have differed from the life without end we may have in that it would have been without the knowledge of good and evil while ours, should we come to have it, will be accompanied by with such knowledge. The divinization made possible by the Fall includes the specific gift of moral discrimination, which is immediately gained by eating the forbidden fruit. This is a felicitous gift, at least in the sense that it provides a good not otherwise to be had. It is also a curse: knowing good and evil carries with it, for Eve and Adam and all human creatures (except Mary), knowledge of one's own incapacity to do the good, and therefore of one's own subjection to the complexes of absence and lack and recursively self-consuming action that we call evil and sin. Noting the felicitous aspects of the Fall's fault doesn't require blindness to its disastrous and lamentable aspects.

There is another indication in Genesis of the felicitousness of the Fall. When the LORD has cursed the serpent and Eve and Adam, each in their respective ways, and made them garments of skin (*tunicas pelliceas*, signifiers among other things of mortality, of the death—*mors*—with which those who wear these clothes are now burdened), the LORD says, "Behold the man (*ecce homo*)" (Genesis 3:22), and goes on to note that the people in question (*homo* here embraces both Eve and Adam; it's generic rather than gender-specific) are those who might, if appropriate precautions aren't taken, seek and find eternal life. The same phrase, *ecce homo*, is used by Pontius Pilate when, in John's Gospel (19:5), he presents Jesus, crowned with thorns and clothed in purple, to the crowd that wants him crucified. Adam is the man who would find eternal life were it not barred to him and had he not received instead the burden of mortality: look at him (*ecce homo*). Jesus is the man who gives eternal life precisely by taking on the burden of mortality in order to overcome it: look at him (*ecce homo*). The verbal echo resonates with an echo in the nonverbal order: Jesus is the second Adam; his work reprises and reverses the work of the first Adam, and the work of the first Adam prepares and makes possible the work of the second. Without Adam, no Jesus; without Jesus, no Adam. The deepest felicity of the fault that is the Fall is that it serves to prepare us for the gifts that Jesus gives and, therefore, for the entire history of salvation. It does this while also submerging us in the ocean of blood and slaughter and suffering and death that begins with the banishment from Eden and the murder of Abel by Cain.

Christians are tempted, and many have succumbed, to extend and systematize the thought that the Fall is a felicitous fault into a doctrine of providence. Such a doctrine might say that the LORD foresees (*pro + videre*, whence "providence") all and ordains all, providing providentially that out of every fault good(s) will come, as the sweetness of honey came from Samson's slaughtered lion. It's possible to go further and say that not only will each fault be linked causally to a good or goods otherwise unattainable but that, in each and every case, this must be so. On such views, providence is a matter of causal necessity given by the LORD's omnipotence and omniscience. This is to subordinate the LORD's love to the LORD's power; it is also to subordinate the blank opacity (to us, that is) of suffering and death to its redemption in glory; and it is to subordinate the crucifixion to the resurrection by over-anticipating the glories that will be apparent to us only after the general resurrection.

All of that is a mistake. It is better, for the purposes of this book, for those of Christian theology, and for those of the Christian life, to resist the temptation to formulate and systematize a doctrine of providence and instead to focus on the clear case and the mode of possibility. Out of the strong (Samson's lion again) came forth sweetness; out of the Fall came forth incarnation; and out of the incarnation came forth salvation. These felicities are works of love, and opaque ones: Samson's slaughter of the lion belongs to a complex economy of divine gift and human receipt and refusal, opaque to its protagonists at almost every stage and involving massive and systemic violence throughout, as is also true of the trajectory that runs from Fall to the Ascension. This is quite compatible with the presence of real felicities in the events and with the possibility that all faults—all sins, all sufferings, all violences—give birth to felicities as well as to pain and suffering and blood. When faults do come with felicities, when they are in some part felicitous, that is and can only be because the LORD works on them with love by regretting and then transforming them, and even when that is so, and is known by us to be so (two very different things—consider again Samson, an instrument in the LORD's hand almost entirely without understanding of that fact), the felicities in no way erase the fact of the fault, neither in the order of being nor in the order of knowing.

There's a further and sharper point to make about the felicities that flow from the Fall. They aren't given directly to Eve and Adam. Their life after the expulsion from the garden isn't one in which the knowledge of good and evil seem to be much of a blessing. They are, in the scriptural depiction, given a life of unremitting and painful work, he as tiller of the soil and she as bearer of children. They have children, but one of their sons inexplicably murders another. And the only thing scripture has to say about Adam's death is that he lived for 930 years and then died. (It says nothing about Eve's death, which is another of the significant parallels between Eve and Mary.) There's no hint of felicitousness in any of this. There's only work and pain and loss and death. The felicities that come from their Fall belong to others. Or so it seems.

There's an ancient (perhaps as old as the second century) Christian tradition that, on the Saturday separating his Friday death on the cross from his Sunday resurrection from the dead, Jesus descended to hell, the place of the dead, and took out of it those among his progenitors judged worthy to be with him in his resurrected and ascended life—which might mean everyone. Among those often depicted in Christian art as being so taken are Eve and Adam: there are affecting images of them holding the fingers of Jesus's outstretched hand as they're taken out of hell and moved toward heaven. Without pressing the details of the tradition (there are many interesting difficulties about it), it can be taken to show that Eve and Adam did, eventually, receive the felicities and blessings that flowed from their Fall—that is, they received Jesus. Suppose that's right. (I suppose that something like it is.) It remains the case that, first, Eve and Adam are not the only or the first or the principal recipients of the blessings given by their Fall, and, second, that the felicities they did receive weren't given to them in this life but only after death. For both these reasons we should say that there's a loose link, for them, between the Fall and its felicities and that their eventual receipt of those felicities in no way removes, nor even reduces, the regrettability of the Fall's occurrence. What they did in the garden remains a *culpa* no matter the degree and kind of its consequent felicities; it should therefore be regretted and lamented by them and by us. Among the things we should do when thinking about their Fall and our replications of it is to say, emphatically and repeatedly, "I would it were otherwise." That is so, no matter how felicitous these falls may also be.

I've been writing as though it's essential to the grammar of Christian thought to say that there was a first couple, our first parents. And in one way that's so: this is what Christians say, and we say it because scripture says it and because there's a long Christian tradition of saying it and elaborating upon it. Already in scripture, for instance, there's evidence of thought about Mary as the second Eve and Jesus as the second Adam. That way of thinking and talking cannot easily, and perhaps cannot at all, be abandoned by Christians. But that's different from making any claim about the existence, space-time location, or genetic makeup of Eve and Adam. Those are questions that belong to a different register, and I here take no position on them other than the descriptive one that taking positions on them has been of at best marginal relevance to Christianity. Thinking about Eve and Adam has other functions for Christians, and the one of interest here is that it provides a focus for analysis of what properly (necessarily) belongs to human creatures. What we talk about when we talk about Eve and Adam is themselves, certainly, but also ourselves. Their humanness is also ours, by inheritance and participation, and when we depict their Fall, we show something about our own and about the nature and effects of such falls in general. In this instance, what's theirs is inscrutable sin (the Fall) from which both damage and felicity flow; they also show us that neither all the damage nor all the felicity produced by particular sins belongs to those who did them. We, like they, can damage the world and participate in its healing both temporally downstream and temporally upstream of the acts by which we do these things. Eve and Adam's Fall damages the world far downstream of itself and themselves, and it participates in the healing of that damage, healing which is Jesus, and healing which also reaches back, far upstream of its temporal location, back to Eve and Adam themselves, and behind and before them to the fallen angels. We, like they, can find room made for unanticipated felicities by our sins; we, like they, should resist the thought that regret (remorse, contrition, penitence) for our sins is unnecessary because of those felicities; and we, like they, should renounce the thought that every felicity that has room made for it for by our sins is for us.

It's easy enough to see that the thought "I would it were otherwise" and the thought "a very good thing came from it" are easily compatible and that in some cases it's very important to hold them together. Imagine that in your twenties you married someone deeply unsuitable for you—perhaps (s)he was crazy, duplicitous, manipulative, already married, about to be jailed, violent, or what have you. You married this person for bad reasons, whatever they may have been, and the marriage goes badly. After a decade it ends in acrimonious divorce. You are convinced the marriage was a mistake. You regret it deeply. You wish it otherwise in one or many ways—by wishing that you'd married a different person, that the person you did marry hadn't been as (s)he was, that you hadn't been as you were, that you hadn't married at all, . . . and so on. But. The marriage yielded children, and you love them dearly. You don't wish them otherwise. You think of them as something as close to an unmixed good as there is in this world. You acknowledge, too, what is obvious, that without the regrettable marriage, these children would not exist. Can it then make sense to wish the marriage otherwise? It can. It was a *culpa*, a culpable fault, to have married that person. You should have known better, and in some sense, even when you married, you did know better. Your reasons for marrying were all bad (that can never quite be true, but let's allow it for the sake of the example) and so the marriage was a mistake you're right to be remorseful about. The children, though, were and are felicities in something like the way, though on a very much smaller scale, that Jesus is a felicity of the Fall. Your recognition that the marriage was a mistake and that you wish it otherwise is well-formed and need not at all call into question your thought that your children are blessings. Similarly in the reverse direction, your recognition that your children are felicities need not at all call into question your understanding that your marriage was a regrettable mistake. And there are strong advantages to this way of cutting the cake so far as the grammar of Christian thought and the living of the Christian life are concerned—not least that preserving and nurturing regret for what's regrettable permits an otherwise-impossible transfiguration of those states of affairs.

The marriage example involves culpability. There are also many states of affairs that are properly the objects of otherwise-attitudes that involve no culpability. Suppose you're fourteen, bursting with mathematical and musical talents. It's clear to those who teach you that you have the talent and energy to be successful as a concert pianist or as a pure mathematician. But no one thinks—you don't yourself think—that you can be both. No one has time and energy enough for both. Either you'll be giving twelve hours a day to emulating Katia Buniatashvili or you will be giving those hours to research in the topology of curved space. The time has come to make a choice, and you make it, for mathematics. Your work at the piano recedes, and your attention to topology intensifies. By thirty-five, you've won the Field Medal and become the holder of a chair in pure mathematics at Stanford, and you're a Sunday pianist, playing for your own pleasure and that of your intimates, but you're far, very far, from being a top-drawer concert pianist. That, now, you'll never be. In your seventies you look back with sadness and some regret at the possibility lost. It's not that you think you made the wrong choice. You think it right that a choice had to be made, and you're happy that you've been able to make significant contributions in mathematics. But you regret a real loss, the loss of the good of a piano life of a degree of excellence you'll never now reach. You wish that loss otherwise. Are you mistaken in doing so? Perhaps not. It's a real loss of a real good, supposing you're right about what was possible for you in that sphere. What you're wishing otherwise is an aspect of finitude: because you lacked the time, you couldn't do a good thing that otherwise you might have done. Whether your regret is appropriate in this case depends on whether that kind of finitude—the kind that makes us, perhaps definitionally, incapable of realizing all the goods we could have realized were we not limited in this or that way—is a lack in us or, rather, an essential feature of what we are. That's a question beyond the possibility of resolution here. All that's needed at this point is the commonplace that we do, and prima facie ought to, wish otherwise states of affairs for which we are not culpable — and for which, perhaps, no one is culpable.

The Shoah is a third case of something to be wished otherwise while acknowledging that good things came from it. Among those felicities are works of literature (Paul Celan's poetry), film (Claude Lanzmann's *Shoah*), and visual art and architecture (Yad Vashem) that without it would not have come to be. There are political changes (the State of Israel), and perhaps some changes in the rhetorical norms of the West (it is, post-Shoah, more difficult for forgeries such as *The Protocols of the Elders of Zion* to find a credulous audience than it was before), that would not have happened if the Shoah had not occurred. And there are acts of courage and self-sacrifice prompted by the Shoah's violence. These are all felicities, even if none of them are without ambiguity — there are no unambiguous felicities in the human sphere since the Fall: Celan committed suicide; the State of Israel has killed and displaced many; Lanzmann's film is as often as not heavily portentous. Nevertheless. There are real felicities here, and they have a lamentable horror as their occasion. "Regret" is much too light a word for the intensity with which I wish the Shoah otherwise; I might even say that I am contrite for my part in it, even though it was over more than a decade before I was born. The Shoah's downstream felicities don't in any way or to any degree moderate the necessity of having and showing, with respect to it, the attitude encapsulated in the thought "I would it were otherwise." The extreme nature of the example makes clearer the necessity of holding together affirmation of downstream goods with unambiguous and unmoderated lament-regret-contrition for the horror that made those goods possible. This isn't easy to do. We naturally and almost inevitably think that acknowledging the presence of some goods in a state of affairs ought to moderate the intensity with which we wish it otherwise or wish it out of existence. But there is no good reason to think this. If the state of affairs in question is the complex wanton-genocidal-murder-of-six-million-Jews-coupled-with-the-downstream-felicities-flowing-from-that-genocidal-murder, then we wish otherwise — which here must mean wishing *not* — the genocidal murder while celebrating, with reservations, the felicities that have come from it.

A DISTINCTION SUGGESTED EARLIER NOW NEEDS TO BE RETURNED to. It's the distinction between the possibility that faults can produce felicities and the necessity that they do. If the former is the case, then it's possible that some faults may be pure in the sense that no felicities of any kind flow from them. If the latter is the case, then no matter how flagrant the fault, some felicities will inevitably flow from it. Both of these paths of thought have been followed by Christians, and which of them is taken has significance for how regret and other otherwise-attitudes are understood to work.

Advocates of both views should agree that whether or not it's necessary that all faults bring felicities with them, it's certainly the case that there are faults whose damage is not directly redressed by any felicities they cause. This is most obvious in the case of damage done by human creatures to one another. If I kill or torture or rape or otherwise injure you, and there are some felicities that flow from my act, it needn't be the case that those felicities are evident or comforting to you, the one who suffered the wrong I did you. Ordinarily—or at any rate much too often—there is nothing redeeming or transfigurative for ourselves in what we suffer at the hands of others. Too often, what we suffer leads us to die in darkness and agony, broken and unredeemed. Or we die suddenly and without occasion for preparation, too soon, without a future we might have had. Or we die without ever having become conscious, dismembered in the womb. Christians say, and I too want to say, that there is a postmortem future for those who die in these ways, a future in which they may find both peace and glory. But that peace and that glory, no matter their intensity and no matter their endlessness, do not and cannot erase, much less make up for, such sufferings. An endless life of intimacy with the LORD, gift of unparalleled beauty and delight though it is, is not the kind of gift that brings the history of those who receive it to nothing. Rather, their history is taken up into that new, gifted life, there to remain, transfigured in something like the same way that Jesus's wounded natal flesh, tortured by crucifixion, is taken up into his resurrected and ascended flesh, which is still marked with wounds even though they no longer bleed. It's a commonplace of the Christian archive to say that the resurrected flesh of the martyrs is marked with the wounds of their martyrdom, which is another version of the same point. Christian depictions of the resurrected Jesus and Christian martyrologies could have moved in the direction of erasure, of depicting the risen Jesus as wound-free, but they did not, and they didn't because the view that damage is erased by healing is sub-Christian, if too often espoused by Christians. This isn't to say that Christians have always given the same significance, either in representation or devotion, to the wounds of Christ, or to their analogues in the flesh of the martyrs. Sometimes devotion to the wounds has become baroque in detail and intensity, and sometimes it has receded to the horizon. But the wounds have never quite gone away, and they cannot so long as the practice of Christianity remains.

The properly Christian taxonomy of damage done in this age of the world, between creation and eschaton without respect to the life of the world to come, then, is this: there is damage that brings some felicity to those who suffer it (whether by what they do to themselves or by what is done to them by others or the world) and there is damage that brings no felicity to those who suffer it. There is, I expect, though there is no way to tell for sure, much more of the latter than the former. If we extend our gaze beyond the confines of the life of this world to that of the world to come, then new difficulties arise, consideration of which extends beyond the scope of this study. If, as I take it, though here without argument, universalism is true, which is the same as to say that after death there is only heaven, even though a heaven that will appear purgatorially to most for a time, then it is the case that all damage, all suffering, will eventually bring felicities with it for those who were damaged. These postmortem felicities, though, aren't compensatory and don't erase the damage from which they came; they transfigure it, fully, but that is far from the same thing. The pain of that damage, its futility, *alles umsonst*—all for nothing—as Walter Kempowski solemnly, beautifully, and aphoristically puts it in his final novel (*All For Nothing*), remains always, as a feature of the cosmos. At least, this is so once the nature of time is properly understood. Heaven makes nothing go away, in the double sense that, first, nothing is exactly what it does make go away (sin and evil and death are, strictly speaking, nothing) and that, second, nothing that is, is lost there. Rather, heaven transfigures everything. The thought "I would it were otherwise" continues, as a bassline, even when the *Sanctus* is sung by the saints in heaven. It's a non-bleeding wound in the melody, until the end of the age.

But still it remains to address the question of necessity. Do felicities inevitably flow from faults? Or is it possible that there can be felicity-free damage? Thinking about the LORD yields an approach to an answer. The LORD's regrets are all about felicity: their occurrence is the means by which damage is healed, and because the LORD is the LORD, all damage is both healable and (atemporally) healed. The Fall's felicities bring salvation, which is the felicity greater than which none can be thought. So far as the LORD is concerned, then, all faults do come with felicities, and necessarily so. To say otherwise would be to make the LORD not the LORD. Once again, though, this doesn't mean that the LORD erases faults. They and their corresponding damage remain what they are. What the LORD does is transfigure them, bring from them felicities that otherwise would not have been. The essentials of the position can be put, abstractly, in the atemporal-present tense: faults, with their damage, occur; the LORD necessarily transfigures those faults and heals that damage.

The difficulty that remains for us, individual sinners and sufferers that we are, is about the demarcation of damage—the individuation of one instance from another. Suppose I come to learn that my agonizing suffering and imminent death from ebola is instrumental in the development of a vaccine against that disease. And because of that vaccine, soon no one will need to suffer from ebola. That won't alter the fact that I'm suffering from it now and will shortly die in agony. Setting aside the psychological aspects of this situation (I may or may not be comforted by the knowledge of the felicities that will flow from my suffering), different decisions about how to demarcate one instance of damage from another yield different conclusions about the inevitable transfiguration of damage. If my ebola-suffering is an instance of damage properly distinct from ebola-suffering in aggregate, then the conclusion is that not all damage is healed because the felicities that flow from some instances of it may affect only other instances.

If, on the other hand, ebola-suffering is understood in aggregate as a single thing without proper parts, then the conclusion is that all of it is transfigured—just as, by analogy, when my impacted and painful wisdom tooth is extracted and the infection has yielded to antibiotics, then it's attractive to say that my infected tooth has been healed.

There's no obviously correct way to demarcate one instance of fault or one instance of damage from another. This means that there's also no obvious way to answer the question of whether every instance of damage is healed and whether every fault brings felicities with it. What the grammar of Christian thought requires is that the following claims be held together: (1) the LORD brings felicities out of all faults; (2) the LORD heals all damage; (3) there are apparently particular faults from which no felicities flow; (4) there are apparently instances of damage that remain unhealed. Holding those claims together yields the characteristically Christian complex attitude to fault and damage, which is lament-laced hope. We hope for the felicitous healing of all faults with their concomitant damage; we lament the massively evident presence of fault and damage in the world, together with the equally massively evident presence of unfelicitous faults and unhealed damage here. That complex attitude, with its concomitant practices, is essential to Christianity—of first-order significance. Resolution of the tension between the first and second pair of claims is, comparatively speaking, of minor significance, and it can be done in various ways. My preferred solution is to take universalism with respect to salvation (hence, serene hope) and realism so far as fault and damage are concerned (hence, lament), and to combine both with modesty about our capacity to individuate states of affairs and to demarcate instances of fault or damage one from another. Our otherwise-attitudes—remorse, regret, contrition, compunction, and so on—are intimate with realism about fault and damage; the extent to which that realism is required of Christians is the extent to which otherwise-attitudes also are.

CHAPTER THREE

Time

Ordinarily, our otherwise-attitudes are directed toward the past, whether to events belonging to our own past (things we have done or failed to do, things done to us) or to events and states of affairs prior to or in some other way, as we see them, independent of ourselves (the last dinosaur's last sigh, the trail of tears, the adoption of agriculture by human creatures). It's easy enough to see why this is so: it's a grammatical fact about the verbs (in English) that indicate otherwise-attitudes that they refer to the past. When you say "I regret that p," or "I'm remorseful about q," or "I've learned that I need to be contrite about r," your hearers will assume that the states of affairs you're talking about—whether they're events, actions, or complexes of both—occurred in the past. This assumption is almost as strong, and almost as hard to resist, as the one that'll make your hearers think that p is something yet to happen when you say "I anticipate p."

But it is not quite as strong. It is possible to give sense and purchase to "I regret that p" where p isn't past but, rather, future or present. You might, for example, reasonably say that you're contrite about the fact that this time next month you'll have been divorced (the future perfect tense is the one you'd use for that), or you might say that you are contrite about the fact that by midnight you'll be drunk again. It's not so easy to give plausible instances of p in "I anticipate that p" that make of p a past, or completed, state of affairs. The connection in speech and thought between otherwise-attitude verbs and

past-completeness is strong, but not as strong as that between antici-
pation and future states of affairs.

The connection that is just about as strong is the connection between otherwise-attitude verbs and the inevitability of their objects.
The reasonableness of your thought that you regret next month's divorce or tonight's drunkenness is closely indexed to the likelihood
(to you or to your hearers) that those states of affairs will happen.
If all the paperwork for the divorce has been completed, and you're
waiting only on the judge's pro forma grant of the decree, then you
can regret it, and be understood reasonably to do so, even though it
hasn't happened yet. And if you're a habitual drunkard who's been
intoxicated by midnight every night these past five years, then you
can reasonably regret, and be understood reasonably to regret, tonight's upcoming drunkenness. The reasonability of the locution in
both cases depends upon the likelihood, perceived or real, that the
state of affairs obtains in one or another of the three times. And it's
this connection with completeness that underlies and explains the af-
finity between otherwise-attitude verbs and past states of affairs. The
shape and force of the language we use moves us almost irresistibly
in the direction of speaking as though and thinking as if what's past
is completed, frozen in time gone by like Satan in the ice of Dante's
hell. Our patterns of speech and writing suggest to us that what's past
is, ordinarily, inaccessible to change in the same way that an email or
text, once the send button is pressed, can't be recalled.

There is, then, a strong and deep grammatical and conceptual connection between the otherwise-attitudes and the inexorable givenness
of their objects. The strength and depth of that connection is intensified by particular understandings of space and time. If, for instance,
past states of affairs are understood—usually implicitly (few people
have views about these things that they can make explicit)—as paradigmatic of what's given and frozen in its givenness, that's because of
a view, or a family of views, about the nature of the past and its relation to the present and the future. This family of views perceives time
in linear mode. On this view, where you are now, temporally speaking, is the present; behind you, on the timeline, stretches the past, extending backward to an imperceptible vanishing point; and in front

of you, extending forward, perhaps endlessly, is the future. You are, on this view, ineluctably moved (moving) forward into that future and thereby away from the past. You're on a moving sidewalk: it takes you where it's going, and it's going in only one direction. But the timeline is even more forcibly one-way than the moving sidewalk. The sidewalk makes it difficult for you to go against the flow; effort's needed to do that, but it's not impossible. But on the timeline, going backward is strictly impossible. There are cherubim and flaming swords at your back, and they can't be circumvented. They make it impossible for you to go back. The past, on this view, is accessible to you only testimonially (you can hear about it), conceptually (you can think about it), and contemplatively (you can look at it). You can't interact with it in other ways. Most importantly, you can't contribute to its alteration. Time passes, and you're taken along with it.

THIS IS THE COMMONSENSE VIEW. IT'S INTIMATE WITH THE TENSES of our natural languages. And it's articulated with the use of a particular kind of device for measuring time. Such devices make time legible for us in something like the way that maps make space legible for us. Absent such devices, there's only blank illegibility. If you're becalmed on a boat in the open sea, shrouded in fog so that there is no sound and nothing farther away than a yard or so is visible, and you're without compass or GPS device, then space is illegible: you can't read your position because no measures are available. Just so with time. If you're in an isolation chamber with constant temperature and light and no intrusions of any kind, time's passage will be almost illegible for you. "Almost" illegible because you'll still have the measuring devices for time's passage that belong to your flesh—such things as growth of hair and nails or menstrual cycles. Observing these processes, however—running the back of your hand across your chin to assess how many days' growth of beard you can feel, for instance—will not permit much legibility. Perhaps the usual rates of these processes are altered by the isolation chamber in ways that make your past experience of hair and nail growth an unreliable guide. (It's also possible, though less clear, that the flesh absent other spatial measures has some devices of its own for rendering space legible—resonance with the planet's magnetic fields, for example, or with sidereal cycles.) Whatever the case about the flesh's resources for rendering space and time legible, it's certainly true that these resources are severely limited and that the legibility they bring is less precise and textured than what's given by extra-fleshly devices such as the compass and the chronometer.

Devices for measurement make what they measure legible. But they don't do so by holding a mirror up to nature, if by that we mean reflecting without change what's there. Even mirrors don't do that. Rather, measuring devices shape what they measure, and the way they measure makes what they measure seem, to us, to have one shape and not another. Consider, for instance, the difference between the shape time seems to have when measured by a sundial and the shape it seems to have when measured by a clock tick. The former responds to the daily cycle of the sun, and those who read it interpret a repeated lengthening and shortening of solar shadow as the Earth rotates around the sun. The shadow cast by the sundial's measuring rod moves in a circle: in its end is its beginning, just as the sun's setting is the precursor to its rising. Time made legible in this way seems cyclical and beginninglessly and endlessly repetitive. Its geometric representation is the circle. By contrast, the clock tick, made evident in the changing numbers of a timer, is arbitrarily linear: the timer begins somewhen at 00:00 and moves forward at regular intervals (00:01, 00:02, 00:03, . . .) into an apparently endless future. There's nothing intrinsic to clock ticks that suggests an endstop; if there is one, as when a timer is used to measure the speed (time over distance) of a runner on a track, it's as arbitrary as whatever the beginning point was. Legibility in this case is linear and more dramatically artificial (an artifact) than in the case of the sundial. We, the measurers, have made the devices that provide the clock ticks and stipulate the intervals at which the ticks occur; we've probably made the sundial too, but, as it seems to us, what we've made is intimate with and responsive to something we haven't made, which is to say the sun. That's not so, or less obviously so, for clock ticks.

Most devices for tracking and measuring time are somewhere between these ideal types. That is to say that the legibility they provide is in part linear and in part cyclical. A wristwatch, with its circu-lar dial and hands, is more like a sundial than a digital timer, while a smartphone timer's flickering numbers approach the purity of the simple clock tick. But in each case there are vestiges of the other kind of legibility. Most users of wristwatches now, artifacts perhaps ap-proaching the archaism of the sundial as the twenty-first century gathers momentum, see the cyclical legibility of time provided by the watch's circular face and its repeated twelve-hour cycle, but they also find it obscured to some degree by the strength of the linear clock ticks present so prominently elsewhere. And even though telling the time by looking at your smartphone carries few signs of repeated cycles and many signs of beginningless and endless linearity (an im-pression deepened if you consult the calendar function on your phone that typically extends for centuries, and sometimes millennia, in both directions), the time-legibility it provides you is inflected by remnants of circularity, most obviously by its preservation of the twenty-four-hour day, which is a solar-based cyclical measure.

Space also, like time, appears differently to us depending on the devices we use to measure and represent it. Finding your place in the world by satellite-provided coordinates suggests, with almost ir-resistible strength, that space is a flat plain, infinite in its extent, mea-surable by grid, and essentially uniform: the question about where something is can, on this view, be exhaustively answered by specifying the appropriate coordinates. That impression is already strong in the legibility given by two-dimensional maps, but it's been intensified by the advent and wide use of the information provided by global positioning satellites. Space made legible in this way is smooth and regular, and it is without obvious, or any, beginning or end. Opposed to this, and on some readings incompatible with it, is the sense of spa-tial location that most of us have. According to that, there are signifi-cant places (homes, places we've been, sacred places where important things happened) and insignificant ones (places we've not been and have no plans to visit, places where nothing important has happened, deserts and empty spaces, places of devastation). Space's legibility in this way of construing it is a matter of rough ground, mountains and crevasses, safety and danger, limits and bounds, and finding yourself, often, back just where you began even when you've been trying to get somewhere else.

The map grid for space and the clock tick for time are coordinate: they are kinds of legibility that belong together and support one another in showing what they measure as beginningless, endless, regular, frictionless, smooth, and inexorable. Likewise for the sundial and the rough ground: those too are kinds of legibility that belong together and support one another in showing what they measure as repetitive, nonuniform, and porous. The place for pilgrimage and the time of the sacrament resonate with one another, as do global positioning system coordinates and coordinated universal time measures. This intimacy of time and space has been a commonplace of mathematics and physics since the formulation of the general and special theories of relativity early in the twentieth century; it is also, and has been for much longer, a commonplace of Christian thought because of the necessity Christian thought has labored under of distinguishing the LORD from everything that is not the LORD. One way of doing that is to place the LORD outside time and change, a placement that, it was soon seen, also required placing the LORD outside the possibility of spatial movement. It's evident that spatial change, movement from here to there, involves temporal change and isn't possible without it. It's almost as evident that temporal change requires spatial locatedness and that beings, if there are any, without spatial location—which is the same as saying unbodied beings, beings without extension (numbers and propositions and sets, perhaps, and all the entities of mathematics; angels, according to some, though wrongly as I see it)—could not, because of that lack, change at all. Once this pattern of thought was in place, space and time began to be understood by Christians as features of the created order, and coordinately so. Creation was seen as definitively spatiotemporal, and every temporal feature was also understood as a spatial feature, just as every spatial feature was also understood as a temporal feature. The LORD's act of creation, it follows at once, didn't occur in space and time, but, rather, brought into being a spatially and temporally extended order. To be extended in that way is exactly what it means to be a creature.

CHRISTIANITY HAS ITS OWN PECULIAR DEVICES FOR MEASURING space-time and thus for making it legible. Principal among these is the liturgy, the Christian people's worship of the triune LORD we confess. Liturgical activity is fundamentally and essentially repetitive and cyclical: it is, that's to say, endlessly repeated, and it finds its end in its beginning and its beginning in its end, like the worm Ouroboros. The legibility it gives to space-time is therefore in every important respect unlike that provided by the clock tick. Christian liturgical celebration shows space-time's circularity and rhythmic repeatability by emphasizing its participation in eternity, which is to say in the LORD; correspondingly, it makes porous the boundaries between the past, the present, and the future.

Consider, for example, the central Christian liturgical act, which is the Eucharist. In that rite, Jesus's ascended flesh, veiled as bread, and his blood, veiled as wine, can be touched and tasted everywhere and at once, without constraint by the metronome of time or the map grid of space. Christians can and do adore and receive his ascended flesh and blood simultaneously in Lomé and London, Chennai and Chicago, Tokyo and Tallahassee, and even while orbiting the planet Earth. This is a strange state of affairs. Catholic doctrine requires the simultaneous real presence and availability of Jesus's ascended flesh to the lingual and manual caresses of his worshipers in widely separated space-time locations, all of them more or less distant from the location of that flesh in its natal form as Jesus of Nazareth in Israel more than two millennia before the time at which I write these words. Formally speaking, it must be the case that the ascended flesh isn't subject to metronomic time or map-gridded space, which is at least to say that what by clock tick is past can be at hand now, in what by clock tick is present. The past is available to us, chronically clock-ticked though we are, no less directly than the present, and that availability extends to the future. The same is true of spatial distance: what takes time to traverse according to the map grid can be had immediately according to the liturgy.

Christian liturgy doesn't (yet) delete the clock tick and the map grid. Mass is still advertised as beginning at 11:15 at the Church of St. Joseph in Bryson City, North Carolina, and the faithful expect it to be over by 12:30 or so, and they complain if it isn't. But what happens at Mass is nevertheless definitively outside the clock tick. The clock tick is provisional and on the way to abolition (it will be abolished in heaven), but it remains in force so long as death does, and for the same reason: the world's healing isn't yet complete—the general resurrection hasn't yet occurred—and so the ending of life in death is still with us and the tick of the clock is what marks, measures, and makes legible that progression. Clock-ticked and map-gridded space-time is the correlate and the measure of death; just as death is what life comes to when it's damaged, so the clock tick is what time comes to when it's damaged. Each is an artifact of the Fall. The liturgy, with the Mass at its heart, shows what space-time is like when healed. That healing includes the breakdown of the rigid boundaries separating, according to the clock tick, the past from the present and the future.

One instance of that availability is that, sacramentally speaking according to the space-time of the liturgy, past states of affairs that you'd prefer to be otherwise are available to you for transfiguration in the present. That is the work of the sacrament of penance.

In 1928 Robert Frost published, in a volume of the same name, a seventy-five-line free verse poem called "West-Running Brook." It has the form of a dialogue between husband (Fred) and wife (unnamed) about a brook. She has twenty lines, he forty-six, and the remaining nine are in the poet's voice. She observes that a brook nearby runs west rather than east (water generally flows east in New England where the poem seems to be set and where it was certainly written), and she likens its opposition to the norm, the fact that it can "trust itself to go by contraries," to the contrariness that characterizes the couple's relationship. She feels herself addressed—waved to— by a foam-flecked contra-flowing eddy in the stream, and an exchange with her husband about this leads him to offer her a discourse on contraries: "see how the brook / In that white wave runs counter to itself."

The discourse is framed by lines that echo one another: "It is from that in water we were from. . . . It is from this in nature we are from." The doubled "from" in each of these lines suggests both the point of origin, which is the countercurrents (the eastward eddies of the west-running brook), and the process by which they (the couple, and all of us) come therefrom, which is to live a life in a stream flowing down while yet resisting that flow by turning and looking and being upstream. The process by which they (we) come from the current/ countercurrent of the brook is a participation in and an instance of "the tribute of the current to the source." The husband's discourse, sententious in part (Polonius would be pleased), ends with a return to dialogue in which the fact of the words spoken in the dialogue is apostrophized—as, by implication, is the fact of the words contained in the poem together with their being read or being heard. The poem's last words are: "Today will be the day of what we both said." The poem's words, and the words spoken in the poem by the spouses, and the nine lines in the poet's (Frost's) voice, and the speaking aloud or reading sotto voce of the poem by you and me—all these words instantiate and participate in the poem's central theme, which is the effect of regret upon time.

The word "regret" occurs just once in the poem, at the end of a long section whose subject is both existence-as-flow and the water-flow of the westward-running brook the couple is looking at. Here's the section:

> And it is time, strength, tone, light, life, and love—
> And even substance lapsing unsubstantial;
> The universal cataract of death
> That spends to nothingness—and unresisted,
> Save by some strange existence in itself,
> Not just a swerving but a flowing back,
> As if regret were in it and were sacred.
>   (Frost, *Collected Poems*, p. 238)

The poem's couple swims in the beauties of time, strength, and so on, which is to say in something, some substance. But that, the beautiful something, is always being evacuated by its opposite, which is nothing. It "spends to nothingness," for which movement death serves as a governing trope. Nothing is always present in what is, as "substance lapsing unsubstantial." It's not only that light and life and the rest are moved by time toward their absence, not only that a time-like stream bears everything away. It's also the fact that the strength- and tone-filled brook is always, while moving, inflected by, eddying around, the nothing toward which it tends. The brook doesn't begin in plenitude and end with a dying fall in nothingness. At every moment—time is mentioned in the list of good things with which the lines above begin, not as an instrument by which substance becomes unsubstantial—life's light is also dark and, complementarily, life's dark is also light.

Resistance to death's universal cataract is evident (in the order of knowing) and present (in the order of being) in the brook's (and life's) "flowing back," which is later in the poem also called a "sending up" and a "backward motion toward the source," of the existence-brook, which is also life and word. This resistance is the countercurrent, *pratiśrotra* as the Buddhists call it, against the stream or the eddy that looks not westward toward the setting sun but the other way, eastward toward the rising sun. It's the wave that waves back toward its place of origin, and among its names in human life is regret, which is sacred. This backward look is what, in the terms given by the poem, keeps life lively and keeps substance substantial. Without it, there is only death, the unbearable temporal weight of the past moving on to death; with it, there's the maintenance of what "is most us," and the provision of regret as its name is an instance of the thing itself, the configuration of the westward-running brook as a human thing not merely subject to time and death and the weight of the past but always also related to those things as their namer. That counter-running, to return to the opening and closing lines of the husband's discourse, is, trans-temporally, where we were and are and will be from; it is also, when we look at it as the poem's couple does at the brook's eddy-wave, that where "most we see ourselves." The order of being and the order of knowing coalesce in these regret-eddies; when we see them rightly and attend to them closely they serve for us as annunciations. Fred has denied that the brook is saying anything directly to the couple. The countercurrent, the wave, like all rivers and waves, was "made in heaven. It wasn't waved to us." She replies: "It wasn't, yet it was. If not to you / It was to me—in an annunciation!" I hear her saying that Gabriel calls her in this way, lilies in foam-dewed hand, to see the defining and transforming character of her own life and that she, in understanding thus what the river says to her, is accepting the eastward-tending eddy, moving toward the Son. That's a strong reading of Frost's words, but not one that leaves them behind. It isn't the reading her husband gives in the poem of her mention of the annunciation. Such talk, he says, goes "off to lady-land" where men can't follow. And perhaps that's right. The trope he's responding to is, after all, Marian. But his immediately following analysis of existence as regret-eddied does accord, even if less lapidarily, with what his wife takes the white-furled wave to have told her.

IN APRIL 1968, A LITTLE MORE THAN TWO YEARS BEFORE HIS suicide in 1970 at the age of forty-nine, Paul Celan visited London briefly (he then lived in Paris), staying with his aunt on Mapesbury Road. He wrote a poem there on the fourteenth of the month, which was, that year, both Easter Sunday and (the second day of) Passover. It opens like this, in Michael Hamburger's English translation (the poem was written in German):

MAPESBURY ROAD

The stillness waved
at you from behind
a black woman's gait.

A black woman walks down Mapesbury Road, and, behind her, the stillness/silence/quiet (*Stille*) gestures. The second person (*dir*) of the opening line is, perhaps, the poet, but also the reader: you're incorporated into the scene, waved at by silence as Celan is, the silence indicated by his words. Then, after a line space on the printed page:

At her side
the
magnolia-houred halfclock
in front of a red,
that elsewhere too looks for its meaning—
or nowhere perhaps.

Next to the black woman walking along with the gesturing silence there's a magnolia, perhaps measuring time (*Halbuhr*/halfwatch, or halfclock, or maybe even half hour). That ensemble (the woman walking, the street, the time-stretched blooming magnolia, the red) looks for *Sinn*/meaning—or, again, perhaps not ("elsewhere—or maybe nowhere"). The scene is sketched, pointillist-fashion, with its elements disjointed and half-seen, half-obscured, even, exactly by what is shown, which is opaque by design. *Sinn* could be rendered "concept" or "idea" as well as "meaning." The idea in the word is shrouded, half-visible, unmeasured, like the scene to which it belongs. Maybe meaning is being sought somewhere and maybe it isn't; maybe the right thing to do with these lines is to ask what they mean, and maybe it isn't. The reader is suspended. And then, after a line space on the printed page:

> The full
> time-yard around
> a lodged bullet, next to it, cerebrous.

Time-yard (*Zeithof*)? This is an uncommon word in German, probably about as uncommon as "time-yard" in English. *Zeithof* is a word from Husserlian phenomenology, which is probably where Celan got it. There it identifies the copresence of the past and the future in a moment of memory: suppose you're remembering hearing a piece of music; in each memory-moment there's a yard (a *hof*, a surrounding area, a yard as in *Bahnhof*, railyard—this is where Hamburger gets "time-yard") or nimbus (this might be better for *hof*, all things considered) in the musical tone present in each memory-moment provided by the tone that preceded and the tone that (anticipatorily) is to come. There is, then, a temporal halo-nimbus-yard surrounding a bullet in someone's brain. But "next to it"? Next to the ensemble sketched in the preceding verses; and next to the brain; and all time-nimbused or time-yarded to one another in an approximate simultaneity. Silence gesturing and the black woman walking down the magnolia-blooming London street (the opening verses) are time-linked to a bullet in someone's brain. We could note that Celan may have had in mind the assassination of Martin Luther King, Jr., which had happened ten days before this poem was written, perhaps also the assassination attempt on Rudi Dutschke in Berlin three days before. Both these events involved bullets to the head. But the poem doesn't say so. What it does say is that violence and silence are time-nimbused, proleptically and retrospectively copresent. And then:

> The sharply-heavened courtyardy
> gulps of co-air.

The German is equally gnomic and tense. But the realization that "courtyardy" is the English rendering of *höfigen*, and that *höfigen* is derived from *hof* (halo-nimbus-yard), opens the poem up. The reader's gaze is directed by this couplet again toward the time-yard of the previous verse. The poem again brings the London street with its particulars together with the violence of bullets to the brain — these things have/are "co-air," *Mitluft*, contiguous air shared with others — and because of that, "sharply-heavened" (*scharfgehimmelten*). Heaven embraces them and brings them spatiotemporally together. Lastly:

> Don't adjourn yourself, you.

The second person (the poet, the reader) of the poem's first line returns and is ordered, imperative mood, not to adjourn (*Vertag dich nicht, du*) him/herself. The verb could also be rendered "postpone." We, those reading, are (perhaps) being told not to extract ourselves from the spatiotemporal copresence the poem has shown us. What would it be to adjourn/postpone ourselves? To separate, abstract, remove, halt ourselves; to prevent ourselves from seeing the sharply-heavened copresence, time-yarded together, of the redblooming magnolia, the waving silence, and the bloodred brainbullet — all of them looking for meaning somewhere, or maybe in no place, as also are the readers of this poem.

"Mapesbury Road" is a poem about time and simultaneity. Time-language runs through it (halfclock, time-yard), as does the language of copresence (at her side, courtyardy, next to it, co-air). The words of the poem bring past and future into the present and lodge the reader (you) just there, in the middle of that temporal knot. It's not a comfortable place. That the poem was composed at Easter/Passover adds depth to this time-yard. Those are days, like this poem, in which violence, blood, and death are temporally knotted with life—the lodged bullet, cerebrous, with the blooming magnolia.

There are resonances in this poem by Celan, as in much of his work, with the sacramental copresence of the past and the future in the present. Celan shows something of what the sacrament of the Mass is and means, and the *Zeithof*, the time-yard (nimbus, halo), can be read as a poetical condensation and suggestive re-rendering of what Jesus does to the clock tick.

Celan is also capable of showing the violence of the clock tick—its inseparability from death. Consider this untitled piece, composed in January 1968 and published as part of the sequence that begins the volume *Schneepart/Snowpart*, published posthumously in 1971. It contains twenty-two words in German, and twenty-three in English as I here translate:

> Illegibility of this
> world. Everything repeats.
>
> The strong clocks
> hoarsely confirm the timecrack.
>
> You, jammed into your deepest,
> climb out of yourself
> forever.

This world doesn't yield itself to the reader. It can't be construed. It's illegible. The reader's gaze trolling for meaning finds itself resisted, and that's because *Alles doppelt*, literally "everything doubles," but probably better rendered, as here, "everything repeats," or even, "everything again." Those renderings might be preferable because of the shift to time-language in the second verse: the doubling appears to have principally to do with repetition. This doubling/repeating is, perhaps, an element in, or even the principal constituent of, the world's unreadability. Whatever you (you, the reader, are apostrophized in the last verse) look at won't be singular; it will already have happened, and it will happen again. The world's unreadability is mirrored by the poem's: if the world is unreadable (illegible, incapable of construal), then so ought the poem to be, as it is. The reader is given the strongest possible signal in the poem's opening line that this poem won't yield itself: it'll resist being read.

As it does. The shift to time-talk in the second verse, in which the "strong clocks"—those unavoidable time-measurers (the strength-figure makes them dominant, controlling of us, the readers of the poem and those who live in this unreadable world)—open something up, has an air of unpleasant violence. The clocks can't be resisted, and what they do is agree with, justify, yield the right to, confirm, affirm—all possible readings of *geben . . . recht*, here rendered "confirm"—the "timecrack," the time in which or at which a crevasse is opened up. Between what and what? An opening into what? We're not told. But the doubling-repetition of the opening verse lingers here, as does the world's unreadability. The timecrack (*Spaltstunde*) is ingredient to unreadability and to repetition, and the strong clocks are what give that illegibility its justification and force. That they do so isn't pleasant: the clocks' voice is hoarse.

You—the reader, the poet, the audience—appear in the last verse. You're wedged, or clamped, or tightly enclosed (*geklemmt*), here "jammed," into "your deepest." That's a figure of fixity, of frozenness, and not one with a pleasant texture. But the poem ends with movement. You, the wedged one, climb out, out of your fixity and out of time—*für immer*/forever. Is there a connection between the timecrack, the fissure, of the second verse and the climb out of the last one? Perhaps. Perhaps the strong clocks open time so that it can be escaped from. Even if so, what the climber climbs into is still an unreadable world. Time's clock-ticked decay, death-ordered, remains.

IN 1989, THE YEAR HE TURNED FIFTY-NINE, TOMAS TRANSTRÖMER published a collection of poems called, in its English version, *For the*

Living and the Dead. One of the poems in that collection, probably written in the mid-1980s, is called "Vermeer." It is in part a response to that painter's *Woman in Blue Reading a Letter*, though it also mentions his *The Music Lesson.* (In what follows I quote from Patty Crane's rendering of the poem in *Bright Scythe*, pages 130–33; I have no Swedish, and so I don't attempt to discuss the original.)

Vermeer's woman in blue is tranquil, still, pregnant. She stands in a room reading a letter. In front of her is a table with some books on it. Next to it are three wooden chairs upholstered with gold-riveted dark blue fabric. To her right, hanging on the wall, is a large map whose details can't be seen clearly enough to discern what it's of. And in front of her, at the other side of the table she's facing, is the painting's source of light (an open window?) that illuminates her features while leaving her back in deep shadow. The angle at which she holds the one-page creased letter that she's reading prevents the painting's light from shining on it directly, leaving it, instead, in shade, though with a radiance given by the light shining through it. She's intent upon what she's reading, attending to it without moving. The painting is without apparent motion, but it is also, at its leftmost edge, open to the light of a world it doesn't represent.

The poem's first two stanzas (it has seven stanzas with varying numbers of lines, for a total of thirty-three lines) don't mention the painting. They're about the noise of the world that begins "right behind the wall," a wall that might be taken to bound a "sheltered world" in which the noise of taverns and murder and trade and money and war, of "demands heaped on demands / gaping red blossom-cups sweating premonitions of war," is kept at bay. Next to all this, and also open to it, is the quiet, motionless form of the reading woman in blue. The world's noise goes "straight through the wall into the bright studio, / into the second that goes on living for centuries."

In this poem as in many others, Tranströmer is much interested in boundaries that turn out not really to be boundaries because they're porous—boundaries between past and present, death and life, me and you, human and nonhuman. Boundaries, in his work, tend also to be doors or, as in "Vermeer," windows; when they're windows they're open, letting what's outside in and what's inside out. In this case, the implied window in the painting *Woman in Blue Reading a Letter* lets the world of time and change and death into that of eternity—the moment of time shown in the painting that goes on living for centuries. It also, though rather less explicitly, lets the eternal world out into the world of time and change. The porousness of Vermeer's windowed world in Tranströmer's hands means that the letter the woman in blue reads must contain news of the world: it's another conduit of exchange between the two worlds. Eternity informs time and time inflects eternity; neither can be what it is without the other. The woman in the painting is also visibly pregnant, "eight months along, two hearts kicking inside her," as Tranströmer puts it. She is motionless in the picture; but inside her is the future, already present, moving forward in time.

Tranströmer also writes about the chairs in Vermeer's painting:

An unfamiliar blue material is nailed to the chairs.
The gold rivets flew in with extraordinary speed
and stopped dead
as if they had never been anything but stillness.

The chairs upholstered in blue with gold fastenings appear to the viewer's first glance as if they've always been there, just as they are, still and calm and lovely, part of the order of things. But as you look more closely, indications within the frame—the news of the world, the light from outside, the gravid belly—begin to suggest that the room's furniture's apparent permanence is under the pressure of time. Those gold studs had to be placed where they are, and they can be unplaced, replaced, displaced; the world's news may require that the chairs be sold or destroyed (perhaps the letter is a last demand for payment of debt); and the light from the world's windows is, as you look at them, fading the too-luxurious blue of the fabric into something older, cooler, calmer.

Reading Tranströmer's "Vermeer" with (a reproduction of) Vermeer's *Woman in Blue Reading a Letter* before your eyes takes the painting out of its frame and places it into the clock-ticked river of time. The displacement puts you, the viewer-reader, under pressure, a situation that Tranströmer underlines:

The ears ring from either depth or height.
It's the pressure from the other side of the wall.
It sets every fact afloat
and steadies the brush.

What the picture shows to its viewers is not static, but floating under pressure from what's not in the picture. Tranströmer shows Vermeer's act of painting to be similarly pressured: that pressure is what "steadies the brush," and it is like the pressure exerted on your gaze by the back of a three-dimensional object, which is the part of the object you cannot see that affects how you see the part you can see. The pressure shapes the picture, but also you, the viewer, whose ears ring with it. You're pulled toward the painting's wall, and as you are, you are shown something about yourself, about your own location in time and the pressure it places you under:

It hurts to go through walls, and makes you sick
but it's necessary.
The world is one. But walls . . .
And the wall is part of you—
. . . .
The clear sky has leaned against the wall.
It's like a prayer to the emptiness.
And the emptiness turns its face to us
and whispers
"I am not empty, I am open."

Tranströmer's poem nowhere mentions regret or remorse or contrition or repentance. It's not, on its surface, about the thought that things would be better otherwise. But it does show something important about the content and presuppositions of that thought. When you prefer otherwise some state of affairs from the past, the present, or (proleptically) the future, you relate yourself to time in a peculiar way. You acknowledge the openness of events in each of the three times to those in the others. What you regret from the past pressures ("It's the pressure from the other side of the wall") the present and the future, and likewise present- and future-directed regrets pressure the past, the present, and the future. Regret, together with its kin, is an acknowledgment of time's porosity, an acknowledgment for which Tranströmer's depiction of Vermeer's letter-reading pregnant woman can stand as an archetype. If, however, the principal or only mode of otherwise-thinking is lament, then time's porosity is no more than a fact of life about which there's nothing to be done. It is, like death and taxes, lamentable, but given and changeless. On that model, Tranströmer's concluding whisper wouldn't be about openness; it would be about the oppressive weight of the given, showing it as nothing more than a burden to be borne. But regret doesn't have to reduce to lament in this way. It can open even the past to change by prompting penitence and penance and thereby transfiguring what's regretted. "I am not empty, I am open"—yes, when the felicities really implicit in the faults or lamentabilities of the past are allowed to show themselves, as they are in Tranströmer's poem. The (tranquil?) pregnant woman reading her news of the world and having her face made radiant by the light from outside while surrounded by the accoutrements of her prosperity is, as Tranströmer shows her, a prism for regret's transformative possibilities. As are you. As am I. Moths, Tranströmer writes in an early poem called "Lament," are "small pale telegrams from the world." The thought that things ought to be different, when open rather than empty, is such a telegram. What it says can be responded to, which means that in some sense things not only ought to be different but can be, and they are made so by the open thought that they might be. Remorse and regret here begin to open into contrition and penance. The woman in blue reading her telegram-letter, in Vermeer and in Tranströmer, is about to give birth.

Tranströmer's "Vermeer" doesn't suggest that the news of the world found in the letter being read, that moth-telegram from the world, can be made other than what it is. What's written in the letter is written, and the reading woman attends to it as it is written: *quod scripsi, scripsi*, Pontius Pilate said, and it's a motto that applies here. The letter's content won't be made different by her act of reading it. In the same way, the baby in her womb is the baby it is, with the form it has and the future it will have; she will, when the baby is born, have to attend to it as the baby it is rather than some other baby. Her pregnancy does not have the efficacy to change the baby and her reading does not have the efficacy to change what is written in the letter. But both her pregnancy and her letter-reading have another kind of efficacy, which is at least suggested by reading Tranströmer and by looking at Vermeer through him: it is the capacity to transfigure the past and, thus, to have a real effect on what you regret and on what you wish otherwise.

CHAPTER FOUR

Lament

THE ATTITUDE "I WOULD IT WERE OTHERWISE" IS COMMON TO all the otherwise-attitudes. Lament stands at its threshold without quite entering the counterfactual territory in which the developed otherwise-attitudes roam. It is, however, an element in those attitudes, even if with varying degrees of intensity, and so it needs to be briefly treated here. If you lament some state of affairs, let's say, you shed tears for it, you tear your hair and rend your garments at it, you bewail it. Whatever it is you're lamenting seems to you dreadful, horrible, or at least unpleasant, and you respond in the ordinary ways. But you don't necessarily wish it otherwise; you simply find it repellent or worse.

Sometimes the past's configuration, that things happened in the way they did and not otherwise, appears to you neutrally as a state of affairs without positive or negative value. In such cases, you note, when you need to, that things were as they were without lament or rejoicing or any of their kin. That Saturn came to have the number of moons it has is, for me, like that; so are the features of the Akkadian script and the particulars of now-extinct Australasian megafauna. There they are or were, these things, and I can contemplate them with interest but not much else. But sometimes, the past's particularities provoke straightforward lament. I lament the Shoah, the Rwandan genocide, the species extinctions of the prehuman past, and, in general, the apparent omnipresence and unavoidability of violence, death, decay, and destruction. Lament attributes value, negatively, to what's being lamented. But lament for a past state of affairs—like its complement, delight (I delight in Shakespeare's having written *King Lear*, in Olivier Messiaen's having composed the *Quatuor pour la fin du temps*, in the fact and the particulars of the liturgy)—doesn't by itself enter counterfactual territory. It doesn't involve speculation about otherwiseness, about what the world as we find it would be like if this or that horror hadn't happened, or about whether the horror in question needed to have happened. It simply observes the state of affairs with horror, or some analogue thereto.

In a schoolyard brawl more than fifty years ago, my friend's leg was broken. I saw it happen, and at the time I was horrified, and I lamented. Looking back, it seems to me that what I was doing was grieving the fact of the brawl and the breaking of my friend's leg in it, and perhaps also the general violence of the schoolyard and the prevalence of bullying there. I didn't at that time—I was perhaps eleven years old—consider whether that particular brawl was avoidable, whether my friend's presence in the schoolyard that day was contingent. All I did was cry and feel shaken by the fact that the world can be—is—like this. I'd had schoolyard fights myself by then, but they'd been minor: skinned knuckles, a bloody nose. The worst I can recall is head-butting another boy and knocking two of his teeth out, giving myself thereby a cut that needed stitches. This, the breaking of a major limb and the calling of an ambulance, seemed much worse. The event made the world seem to me unstable and threatening. But I didn't, so far as I can recall, enter counterfactual territory. I simply lamented the contours of the territory I found myself in.

Giacomo Leopardi, in his *Zibaldone*, provides an example that makes pointed the difference between simple lament and the opening of the counterfactual imagination that belongs to the otherwise-attitudes:

> Once my mother said to Pietrino, who was crying because Luigi threw his little stick out of the window: "Don't cry, don't cry, because I would have thrown it out myself." And he was comforted by the thought that he would have lost it anyway. (Leopardi, *Zibaldone*, p. 70)

Pietrino suffers something unpleasant: he loses his toy because Luigi, his brother, has thrown it out of the window. Pietrino cries, but he is comforted when his mother tells him that if Luigi hadn't thrown it out of the window, she'd have done so herself. That Pietrino is comforted by this suggests that what's upset him is only in part, and maybe not principally, the loss of his toy. It's rather, or additionally, that the loss seemed to him contingent, avoidable, and unexpected. His brother, let's suppose, suddenly and apparently without reason takes it into his head to throw the toy out of the window. Pietrino is upset because it seems to him that it didn't have to be that way. Luigi could have done otherwise, and if he had, the toy would still be in Pietrino's hands. That the mother's intervention succeeds in comforting Pietrino shows the real object of his grief. If he'd been grieving only the loss of the toy, what she says wouldn't have comforted him because the toy would still have been lost even if its loss was inevitable, one way or another. That he is comforted by what she says shows that he's also, and perhaps principally, crying about the past's contingency and unpredictability, which involves a sense that it might have been otherwise. Pietrino would have preferred his brother not to have taken his toy, and he thinks his brother need not have done so. What his mother tells him leads him to think that he was going to lose the toy anyway, if not because of what Luigi did then because of what she would have done, and if not because of that, then, to extend the point, because of what the world would have somehow conspired to do. Pietrino, convinced now of his loss's inevitability, stops crying. He now has nothing to grieve, and since his crying was regret-produced—intimate, that is, with an otherwise-attitude—he has nothing to cry about. He might still cry about the loss of the toy, but if he did he'd be performing simple lament, not counterfactual regret-grief.

This example (it is subtle, striking, and richly provocative of thought, as is characteristic of much in Leopardi's work) shows something in addition to the difference between simple lament and wishing a state of affairs otherwise. That is, it shows the intimacy between lament and the otherwise-attitudes. The contingency of the world's happenings can itself be, and often is, an object for lament. But that lament—we might call it complex or counterfactual lament—already belongs to the otherwise-attitudes because it is already involved with thoughts about, and regrets for, what those who exhibit it take to be the nonnecessity of what they lament. Pietrino, in Leopardi's example, was already a counterfactualist, and his mother could see that he was, which is why she offered the comfort she did—a kind of comfort it wouldn't have occurred to me to offer; I, in lamenting the breaking of my friend's leg, wasn't, or wasn't yet, a counterfactualist.

Simple lament and its complex, counterfactual cousin aren't always, or even typically, cleanly distinguishable from one another. In most actual (rather than thought-experimental) cases, they're intertwined and symbiotic. I make the distinction between them relatively cleanly here for clarity, as is always the case with these kinds of taxonomic distinctions. They're not straightforwardly descriptive but instead heuristically useful (or not). The example I gave has a double payoff. First, it makes clear that lamenting a state of affairs doesn't require wishing it otherwise: the attitude "how horrible that is" isn't the same as the attitude "I would it were otherwise," even if it's ordinarily the case that the two attitudes are close to inseparable. Second, it makes clear that the otherwise-attitudes in their variety don't have to include lament: you can perfectly well wish some state of affairs otherwise in a relaxed, low-intensity fashion, without remotely approaching lament for it.

THE HEART OF SIMPLE LAMENT IS ACKNOWLEDGMENT. THOSE WHO weep are seeing and responding to a truth (if they're accurately understanding what they're weeping for; it's entirely possible to lament a state of affairs that ought not to be lamented), acknowledging it for what it is, and refusing to avert their gaze from it. This is an important, indeed an essential, element of the Christian life: Jesus does it, with respect to Lazarus's death and to the fate of Jerusalem; Augustine, in his depiction in the fourth book of the *Confessions* of his tear-filled grief at the death of an unnamed boyhood friend and, contrastively, in his analysis in the ninth book of the tears he was at first unwilling to shed but then did shed for his dead mother, shows that, and why, lament is a proper Christian response to the death of friends and beloveds, as well as to the fact of sin and death. From the ninth book, about the death of his mother:

> I wept freely before you [that is, before the LORD] for her and about her, for myself and about myself. I let out the tears I'd held in so that they might flow as much as they wanted, making them support my heart. It found rest on them because your ears were there, not those of some man offering an arrogant interpretation of my weeping. And now, O LORD, I confess to you in written words which anyone who wishes may read and interpret as he wishes; if he discovers any sin in the fact that I wept for my mother for a small part of an hour, that mother who had died before my eyes and had for many years wept for me that I might live before yours, he should not deride me but should rather, if he has any love, himself weep before you, the father of all the brothers of your Christ, for my sins. (Augustine, *Confessions*, 9.12.33)

Augustine's weeping in this instance (it can serve as synecdoche for Christian grief) is centrally a communicative act. It is directed to the LORD, and it communicates both an understanding of some state of affairs and an affective response to that understanding. In this case, the death of Augustine's mother, the understanding is that Augustine has been separated from his mother—from, he says elsewhere, the sweet habit of her company (however sweet the habit he often shows himself eager to break it, for example by leaving Africa for Italy without telling her)—without wanting to be and that this separation is an anguish to him. What's important about lament as here presented isn't that it wishes what it grieves otherwise; no, it's that it shows the one who laments to the LORD exactly as he is, which is to say as one who grieves. It's a form of prayer, or of confession. It doesn't seek anything or ask anything, but simply shows itself. There's comfort in that showing: Augustine writes that his tears support his heart (*substernens eas [lacrimas] cordi meo*), and that this gave his heart peace (*requievit in eis [lacrimis]*) because the LORD's ears were there, in that tearful resting place (*ibi erant aures tuae*). The LORD hears when

Augustine speaks, and in this case his tears do the speaking. What they speak is simple lament, and this utterance — it's broadcast in the Psalms, perhaps their most common attitude — is required of Christians. It isn't, however, otherwise-directed. This is abundantly clear in the *Confessions*, and it's clear, as well, in many of the Psalms. If Christians are to develop otherwise-attitudes, simple lament must be supplemented.

Before simple lament is supplemented, however, and along with its supplementation, Christians need to learn what ought to be lamented and what ought not. That capacity isn't available to us without catechesis; we have to be shown it and we have to learn it. This is true of all human creatures. None of us, for example, laments death without being instructed that we should; it's even clearer that we don't lament the sufferings of others without being shown, repeatedly, that they are lamentable. And for more complex lamentables, the point is still more obvious: my own repeated sins are lamentable, but I had to learn what it was to sin before I could lament them; the ineradicable injustices and violences of our political lives (the sovereign state I live in and am a citizen of was founded on genocide and fattened on slavery, every sovereign state has its own version of these horrors) are lamentable, but with respect to those matters, too, a long process of instruction was needed before I could see these things for what they are and thus lament them.

For Christians, the first and last thing to be lamented is death, along with its subalterns and associates. Teaching this ought to be a central purpose, perhaps the central purpose, of Christian catechesis with respect to lament. Such teaching should communicate that death is the negation of life; that it is the antithesis of the LORD's love; that it is, without remainder, the product of sin, which is why it — death — remains a blankly opaque surd in the causal economy of the world; that the essential thread in Christian response to it is lament; that the extent to which this is forgotten, by naturalizing or celebrating death, is the extent to which Christianity is forgotten; that the events of the three days of Easter show with perfect clarity what death is and what its overcoming is like; and that "death" doesn't indicate only human death, but all death, death of whatever kind wherever in the cosmos it is found. Christian catechesis on the lamentabilia is, at heart, catechesis about death. Some of what Christians understand death to be is evident, as well, to the pagans, and it's also the case that Christians have much to learn from them about the texture of death's opacity—for instance, much in the cemetery- and corpse-meditations commended by Buddhists can be instructively deployed by Christians. But there are also countercurrents in pagan thought in which death is naturalized, often in pastoral-romantic mode, and some countercurrents in which death's abolition by sheerly technical means is sought. These need to be resisted and their incompatibility with the Christian view shown.

But such a catechesis on the lamentabilia has as its first yield only lament. It doesn't necessarily move those who undergo it and learn well from it into the counterfactual territory of the otherwise-attitudes. And lament by itself, essential though it is, ushers in despair—or itself becomes a form of despair—as often as it opens into remorse, contrition, and penitence. Despair is lament's characteristic malformation, the damage proper to it, while the otherwise-attitudes are its proper end—and it is the burden of Christian catechesis on the lamentabilia to show the relation between despair and the otherwise-attitudes.

In 1885 or 1886, a few years before his death at the age of forty-four in 1889, in Ireland, that place of exile than which there is none worse for a certain kind of Englishman, Gerard Manley Hopkins wrote the following sonnet:

> I wake and feel the fell of dark, not day.
> What hours, O what black hours we have spent
> This night! what sights you, heart, saw, ways you went!
> And more must, in yet longer light's delay.
>
> With witness I speak this. But where I say
> Hours I mean years, mean life. And my lament
> Is cries countless, cries like dead letters sent
> To dearest him that lives alas! away.

I am gall, I am heartburn. God's most deep decree
Bitter would have me taste: my taste was me;
Bones built in me, flesh filled, blood brimmed the curse.

Selfyeast of spirit a dull dough sours. I see
The lost are like this, and their scourge to be
As I am mine, their sweating selves; but worse.

(Hopkins, *Selected Poetry*, p. 151)

When he wakes, no light comes to him, even though it's day. Instead, there's the "fell," the heavy, smothering blow, of more darkness, unrelieved, intensified even, by waking. He and his heart—Hopkins likes to apostrophize his heart as a device for observing and commenting on himself, as for example in "The Wreck of the Deutschland"— have suffered through the blackness of the night and will now suffer more "in yet longer light's delay."

In the second quatrain, the poet steps back and comments on his own words. He is a witness to himself, and he is his own interpreter. He doesn't mean, he says, that he has had a bad night with a bad day to follow. No, he has had a bad life, with more of it to come ("I mean years, mean life"), and he likens his poem to a letter unreceived by the beloved ("dearest him") to whom it's been sent. The poem is a dead letter, languishing and rotting in the papery graveyard where all such letters end, and its tone is that of lament, explicitly so called, which in this case means cries unheard. The beloved addressee is the LORD, as well as any beloved who isn't here and won't hear because (s)he "lives alas! away." A lament unheard is one sadder than one heard; Augustine eventually learns to say that the LORD's ears provide the pillow for his tears; Hopkins, here, can say only that his tears are buried unheard and perhaps, though he doesn't say it, they are the more bitterly salty for that.

The two tercets with which the poem concludes turn the screw, tighten the torment. The first observes that the poet is to himself unrelievedly bitter. The tropes all have to do with the sense of taste, and the thing that tastes bitter is himself: "my taste was me." And more:

his bitterness, the bitterness he is to himself, is given to him, decreed for him, by the LORD. It is "God's most deep decree," and it is a curse. He understands himself to be cursed in his flesh as well as in his spirit (the final tercet), because what his spirit does to his flesh, already a "dull dough," is sour it. The spirit makes more intense and more unbearable the flesh's bitterness; a dough inedible without yeast is made nauseating by the yeast of the poet's spirit. The poem ends on a note of unrelieved despair. The poet, like all the damned, has as the content of his damnation simply himself, which is bitterness unrelieved.

The two concluding words of the poem—"but worse"—are a puzzle. What could be worse than to be like all the lost, as the preceding two lines have said, scourged just by being "their sweating selves"? The text can be read to say, and criticized for self-dramatizingly saying, that the poet's damnation-scourging-condemnation is, simply, worse than anyone else's. That could be a high-romantic gesture, Wertherian or Faustian, and if it were it would be repellent. I prefer to hear in "but worse" an echo of a fundamental and essential Christian confession as given by Paul, or whoever was the author of the First Letter to Timothy: "Christ Jesus came into the world to save sinners, among whom I am the foremost (*quorum primus ego sum*)" (1 Timothy 1:15). That confession is called, in the letter wherein it occurs, a *fidelis sermo*, a trustworthy saying *omni acceptione dignus*, that ought to be accepted by everyone. All Christians ought to think of themselves as the first and worst among sinners and, when called on, ought to say that of themselves too. There's nothing else to say of oneself, considered simply as oneself, than that; and to say anything else at all is to place oneself as the Pharisee did when he confessed himself glad to be less sinful than others instead of placing oneself as did the *publicanus*, the tax-collector, who confessed himself before the LORD only as a sinner: *Deus, propitius esto mihi peccatori*—LORD, be merciful to me, a sinner (Luke 18:9–14). Hopkins's claim, if this echo is allowed as proper context, to be like all the lost in being self-condemned to oneself and yet at the same time worse than all the others is, on this reading, just what all Christians say. Each of us, like Hopkins, is an authority on the peculiar savor of ourselves; we can speak to that directly, and if we have Hopkins's literary gifts, we can do so with precision and depth. By contrast, the peculiar savor of the sins of others isn't available to us. If "but worse" is a comparison, it's one that belongs to the orders of knowing and seeming: unless I'm self-righteously self-deceived, I know the measure and number and weight of my own sins, but I lack similar knowledge about yours, and so if I compare mine to yours, in the register of address to the LORD, I must say what (Paul) says in the First Letter to Timothy, and what Hopkins says at the end of this poem. That is, if comparative claims are in play, this is the one we must make. Anything else would be the pride of self-righteousness.

There are, no doubt, psychological interpretations to be offered of Hopkins's condition when he was writing this poem—if, that is, it's read for its autobiographical resonances, as it almost always is. He sometimes provides such depictions of himself, as in this letter to Alexander Baillie, a friend from his time (1863–1867) at Oxford, written in April–May 1885, a time close, perhaps very close, to when he wrote "I wake and feel":

> The melancholy I have all my life been subject to has become of late years not indeed more intense in its fits but rather more distributed, constant, and crippling. One, the lightest but a very inconvenient form of it, is daily anxiety about work to be done, which makes me break off or never finish all that lies outside that work. It is useless to write more on this: when I am at the worst, though my judgment is never affected, my state is much like madness. I see no ground for thinking I shall ever get over it. (Hopkins, *Correspondence*, p. 731)

The last words of the long letter from which these words are taken are: "May 17 '85 and still winter." And still winter—Dublin in May—captures not only the feel of the letter as a whole but also, very likely, the rest of Hopkins's life at that time, in which it didn't cease being winter until his hard death from typhoid three and a half years later. Hopkins says in the letter that he's describing the lightest form of his melancholy; perhaps, then, "I wake and feel" (and "No worst," and

"To seem the stranger," and "(Carrion Comfort)") approaches the heaviest. Light or heavy, the melancholy he points to seems to have been a feature of much of his life and to have intensified during his last years in Ireland. A clinician would say that he was depressed, which is about as illuminating as what Hopkins says, which is that he is melancholic. More precise, and more illuminating, would be to say that Hopkins depicts despair well and perhaps suffered from it. The literal sense of that word, and of its French cognate and etymon, *désespoir*, is hopelessness. It is explicit in "I wake and feel," and it is close to explicit in the letter to Baillie, where he finds no reason to think that he'll ever get over his melancholic anxiety about work. There is nothing, in the poem, outside or external to the sense of being damned to oneself, and in the letter, and in other materials from the same period, there is no outside to the sense of failure at work and at poetry. All of it, the bitterness and the failure, is by the LORD's decree, and if there is any change it can only come, inscrutably, from the same place.

Whether you read Hopkins's late poetry autobiographically or not, the clarity with which despair's horizonlessness is shown in his writings of 1883 and later is remorseless. No exit is visible because the melancholic object (self-damnation, failure as a poet, incapacity to work, exile, and so on) is the only visible one, and so hope vanishes and what's left is, strictly, despair. That is lament's characteristic and most thoroughgoing deformity, and while it is not a Christian sentiment (abandonment of hope is never a Christian sentiment), it is one to which many Christians have been from time to time subject just because it's so intimate with lament, which is an essential Christian act. In much the same way that Christians are moved toward supersessionist anti-Semitism, we are moved toward despair—in both cases because of something good and beautiful in Christianity. Despair is lament that is overthought, over-imagined, and overdramatized, an extension into the theoretic and affective realms of something that rather ought to be a responsive action. The question to which despair is an answer (not the only possible answer) is: How should I imagine my future if lament is a constant feature of it? When Hopkins writes "I see no ground for thinking I shall ever get over it" and "and still winter," he provides an answer to the question. Horizonless despair is what his imagination shows him, and he depicts it. But the fact that all human life is lament-laced (death is all around, failure is everywhere, nothing we can do is undeformed, we devastate all the goods we attempt) requires neither that question nor its despairing answer. That there are always occasions for lament requires nothing more of us than that we lament when those occasions present themselves, as they always will. It does not require that we question them or conclude from our questioning of them, as Hopkins does in these texts, that there is no room for hope. That we so easily, so smoothly and naturally, put our laments to the question in this way is among the strong supports of the view that attention to the feeling-fabric of our own existence is among the artifacts of the Fall. Attention lavished upon that fabric is attention turned not toward reality but toward a spectacle. When we look in that direction, as Hopkins does in "I wake and feel," we do something analogous to what Augustine's friend Alypius reluctantly does when he opens his eyes at the gladiatorial games, as recounted in the *Confessions*. We are dazzled by devastation, whether of violence or of feeling, and it is hard to look away. The longer we look, the more real the spectacle seems; we are frozen by it and drawn to it. Hopkins, even in his last years, doesn't always look that way. His poetry and his prose from those years are as often lyrical in hope as drowned in despair. And even when he is hypnotized by the snake eyes of his own despair, he shows, because of the Spirit's gift of words to him, what that despair is like with such vividness that the spectacle shatters before his words, opening into reality. In doing that (the question of what he thought he was doing is irrelevant here, and therefore so is the objection, accurate as far as it goes, that his despair-texts show no overt sign of what I'm describing), he makes a gift to us of a view of what lament's damage is that also makes clear, contrapositively, what it should be. He cracks despairing lament's closed door open, and what it opens onto is remorse, contrition, and confession — onto the panoply, that is, of the otherwise-attitudes.

CHAPTER FIVE

Remorse

SOMETIME IN THE 1860S, PERHAPS IN 1863 WHEN SHE TURNED thirty-three, Emily Dickinson wrote this:

Remorse — is Memory — awake —
Her Parties all astir —
A Presence of Departed Acts —
At window — and at Door

Its Past — set down before the Soul
And lighted with a Match —
Perusal — to facilitate —
And help Belief to Stretch —

Remorse is cureless — the Disease
Not even God — can heal —
For 'tis His institution — and
The Adequate of Hell —
        (Dickinson, *Poems*, no. 781)

Dickinson begins with a term of art, "remorse." She shows what it is by locating it within the type of which it's a token and by providing the characteristics that differentiate it from other tokens of that type. This is a technique she uses in other poems, notably those about renunciation, crisis, and death. In this case, the type to which remorse belongs is memory, and its character is first-personal. It's an active remembering of laceratingly painful things done in the past by the one remembering them in the present: the memorial presence of departed acts for the one who did them. Those flayed by Dickinson's remorse, as almost all of us have been, recall what they did, wish they hadn't done it, and find no surcease.

Remorse, on this understanding, is memorial commotion, memory awake and astir, disturbingly active, restlessly and painfully so. Remorseful memory shows you in bright relief—lighted with a match—what you've done. Your past acts aren't passively present, as on a screen or the pages of a book or a canvas hung on a wall. They're not contemplated restfully as a Stoic or a Buddhist might, noted dispassionately from a distance with the proper label applied, and in that way rendered powerless, or at least less powerful. Rather, they force themselves on you, at window and at door, pressing themselves forward with urgency sufficient to make it impossible to ignore them. The tropes Dickinson uses are, for us, filmic: shot from inside a room, the camera shows a press of forms and bodies at the windows, garishly lit and loud; they crowd, clamoring, the door, as well, which is open or at least ajar, and they're in motion, pressing in, almost inside. You, the watcher, recoil and retreat, but you can't keep them at bay. They're there, all too audible, visible, smellable, touchable, tasteable. Their embrace is fiery; it burns you to the bone, but there's no sanctuary. What's pressing upon you is your own past.

Remorse makes it easy to see these visitors from your past: things you did, things you said, things you thought, things you imagined, persons you hurt, damage you brought about, loss you inflicted, sins you committed, pains you inflicted. Remorse makes perusing these visitors easier and avoiding them impossible. As long as remorse is with you, these spectral visitors are there too, and it's hard not to hear the fifty-first Psalm echoing here in the seventeenth-century English Dickinson would have known ("for I acknowledge my transgression: my sin is ever before me"). But the acknowledgment in Dickinson's poem is unwilling, whereas in the psalm it's part of a longing for forgiveness. Dickinson's remorseful ones can't long for that. They would rather not look at what remorse shows them. However present the memories are, however forceful and lively, the remorseful ones are unwilling to believe in them, unwilling to peruse them, unwilling to credit that they could have thought, said, and done these things and that these visitors might therefore be real. Dickinsonian remorse forces that acknowledgment upon those unwilling to make it. It helps belief to stretch toward recognition, toward the acknowledgment of these departed acts. Yes, you say, forced to it by remorse's flesh-tearing bite (from Latin *mordere*, what rats' teeth do to flesh), I did these things, it's a horror and a wound that I did. It's a stretch to say so, but you're being stretched on remorse's rack and can't avoid saying it. The throng at the door is real and won't go away: you lied to them, you defrauded them, you raped and abandoned them, you enslaved them, you destroyed their reputations with gossip, you coveted and killed and withheld from them, your beloveds as you called and perhaps supposed them, everything of yourself that could have been given to them as a gift. They throng you, and you can neither deny nor ignore them. Your belief has been stretched by remorse and now you can see the truth and it is unbearable.

Dickinson's third stanza adds endlessness to agony. Remorse is cureless, without remedy even by the LORD, because it's the LORD's own device: "'tis His institution." Once remorse is present, once its flensing has begun, once the faces and voices of those you've damaged by your departed acts surround you and press themselves upon you, there's no cessation. They're with you always, endlessly stripping your skin from your flesh, laying you open by laying you waste. Remorse, so understood, is "the Adequate of Hell"—like to, of the same kind as, hell itself.

It's possible that this use of "adequate" as noun is Dickinson's coinage. It is, in any case, so striking a word here as to freeze the eyes. Can she mean it? That remorse's gnawing pain is peculiarly appropriate to hell? Yes. So saying is appropriate to the poem as a whole. If hell's pains are, as classically understood, unbearably intense while yet of necessity borne, and endless, then cureless remorse is indeed paradigmatic of them for it directs the sufferer, the remorseful one, to an unchangeable past in one direction—the past in which the things for which remorse is felt were done, the past in which they cannot change, and the past from which they will forever importune—and to an endless future, always more of the same, in the other. Not, then, merely adequate to, fitting for, hell and not even one adequate of hell among others, but, rather, *the* adequate of hell, the condition in which hell's nature is most fully and perfectly evident. Dickinson seems to have been aware of the oddity and intensity of "adequate" as noun at this culminating point of her poem, and her manuscript shows that she considered, but probably did not finally prefer, "complement." On that weaker text, remorse completes or fills up hell, perhaps by setting off or ornamenting the other components of hell as a red rose complements a silver vase. This too is a strong claim, but calling remorse the adequate of hell is much stronger.

Dickinsonian remorse is a commonplace instance of the counterfactual imagination. Its simplest form is the wish that you hadn't done what in fact you did. That is present to Dickinson's remorseful ones. Their pain is given by that attitude: their past acts accuse them, and they acknowledge the justice of the accusation. That's the only thing present in Dickinsonian remorse. They lament those past acts, perhaps, but they lament more the pain caused by them now, and they wish that pain, and therefore also its origin, away. There's nothing in this of the more complex forms of the counterfactual imagination, in which you not only wish that you hadn't done what you did—and, concomitantly, regret the pain produced by the awareness that you wish you hadn't acted as you did, Dickinsonian remorse is inevitably layered in this way—but also imagine what the world and yourself would be like if you hadn't acted as you did. When you do that, the counterfactual imagination takes up not only the eraser but also the pencil: it begins to sketch what you might have done had you not done what you did, and it pictures how the world would have been different. This isn't present in Dickinson's poem, and that, in large part, is why remorse is so exitlessly, pitilessly painful in it.

Wishing past actions otherwise is never merely an attitude toward the past. Even in Dickinson's poem, remorse includes reference to the present and the future as well. The thronging presence of your past actions, at window and at door, happens now, in the endless present of the poem. And because that present is endless—cureless—it extends also into the future. Dickinsonian remorse belongs to all three times. That can be true, too, of the more complex forms of the counterfactual imagination. Regret for the past may be interlaced with regret for the present and the future: you may be remorseful not only about your past adulteries but also about the fact that you'll continue in them, so far as you can tell (your sense of this may approach certainty), in the future. That is proleptic or anticipatory regret, and it may be as painful as Dickinsonian remorse. When the more complex counterfactual imagination, in which you don't merely wish something away but also sketch to yourself its replacement, is turned toward the future, it can suggest a course of action that would make those future regrettables otherwise and may even, though more rarely, be instrumental in motivating action that does make them otherwise.

Suppose yourself an inveterate and imaginative liar; suppose, too, that you're remorseful about your past lies and that you anticipatorily regret your future ones. But your mendacious habits go deep and you can't see a way to change them quickly and easily. The depth of your remorse directed toward both the past and the future is such, however, that you're prepared to try difficult and long-horizon courses of action to alter your habits. And so you confess your condition, take advice, enlist help, and begin the work of establishing new, truthful habits. In this case your remorse and regret have done something for and to you; they've made you penitent, pricked you with compunction, and made it plausible that some part of the counterfactual country's territory may be transferred from there, where it is only imagined, to the country of the real, where it can be walked around in and enjoyed. You might, gracefully, come to be someone who needn't proleptically regret your future lies, as well as someone for whom the remorse prompted by your past lies is no longer only painful because it is now also a contributor to a better future.

Dickinsonian remorse is not of that kind. It prompts nothing but suffering, provokes no imagination of a future in which its agonies become less intense, and is incompatible with penitence and compunction. It does nothing to those who suffer it other than to make them suffer it, which is why it's the adequate of hell. There's no exit from it. Dickinson is right that this attitude exists. She is right, too, that there are things each of us has done, damage each of us has wrought by our actions, that cannot be erased. She shows what awareness of that is like—how it seems to those who live within the closed horizon of that peculiar kind of remorse. But that is not the whole story. Regret sometimes permits a transfiguration of the past by an opening up of the future. The past is never simply given, unchangeable; its presence to and in the present and the future belongs to it, and when the mode of that presence changes, so too does the past. Dickinsonian remorse contains, and can contain, no transfigurative movement, but it is not the only mode of considering otherwiseness.

IN 1902, WHEN HE WAS FIFTY-NINE, A FEW DECADES AFTER THE composition of Dickinson's poem, Henry James wrote a short story called "The Beast in the Jungle." It belongs to his mature period (he completed *The Golden Bowl* two years later) and it has elements of gothic that make it kin to *What Maisie Knew* (1897) and *The Turn of the Screw* (1898). It's overwrought and oversubtle, but it is also extraordinarily acute about a certain kind of otherwise-attitude, best characterized as remorse, and is, as is typical for the James of this period, polished and precise in technique: it shows readers enough to make them see more deeply into the protagonist's state of mind and fabric of life than he is depicted as doing himself, but not enough to remove the story's narrative tension. And in spite of its gothicisms and its excessive ornaments, the story retains the power to shock.

The protagonist is a man, John Marcher. His foil, and his obscure object of desire, is a woman, May Bartram. They meet first when he is twenty-five and she twenty. He, unprompted, tells her at that first meeting what he takes to be the central secret of his life, which is that he expects—knows—that his life is to be disturbed—overcome, upset, overset, ruined—by some catastrophe. He doesn't know the catastrophe's particulars, but he is certain of its coming. It stalks him, silently and unobserved, like a beast in the jungle, and eventually, he is sure, it will spring.

Ten years later the two meet again. He hasn't thought much about her in the intervening decade and has forgotten that he'd told her his secret. A significant thread in the story is his opacity to himself: he doesn't know why he told her the secret to begin with and can't recall later that he has. She reminds him of what he'd told her ten years before. She hasn't forgotten it, and in this, as often, she is his complement, the one who completes his knowledge of himself while knowing herself better than he does. He, by contrast, is the one who doesn't see even when he's told. He can see neither her nor himself.

Following that second meeting, they begin to keep company as friends, bloodlessly and calmly, and continue to do so for a long time, two decades perhaps. Each is financially independent without being rich, and each lives a life of peace and order in the midst of the kind of beauty that can be arranged by impeccable taste combined with enough money (this is a standard Jamesian theme from *The Portrait of a Lady* to *The Spoils of Poynton*). Each is in a small way a collector of beautiful things, and the time they spend together mostly has to do with that or with other small aesthetic pleasures. Eventually, she becomes ill with the kind of wasting disease typical of women of her class and tastes at that time—at least in literature, and perhaps also in life. Prompted by her illness, she tells him that she knows, now, the particulars of the dreadful thing that was to happen to him. The scene in which she tells him this is also the scene in which the beast makes its leap:

> [He said] "Then something's to come?" She waited once again, always with her cold, sweet eyes upon him. "It's never too late." She had, with her gliding step, diminished the distance between them, and she stood nearer to him, close to him, a minute, as if still full of the unspoken. Her movement might have been for some finer emphasis of what she was at once hesitating and deciding to say. (James, *Complete Stories*, p. 526)

The beast hasn't yet sprung, and it's not too late to prevent it doing so. But, as James's readers have already begun to see, pages before this climacteric, the beast is between and with the two of them, John and May; they are the jungle in which it stalks, and her move toward him—"she stood nearer to him, close to him"—is an attempt to deny it any space between them, which would close off the possibility of its leap. However,

He had been standing by the chimney-piece, fireless and sparsely adorned, a small, perfect old French clock and two morsels of rosy Dresden constituting all its furniture; and her hand grasped the shelf while she kept him waiting, grasped it a little as for support and encouragement. She only kept him waiting, however; that is, he only waited. It had become suddenly, from her movement and attitude, beautiful and vivid to him that she had something more to give him; her wasted face delicately shone with it, and it glittered, almost as with the white lustre of silver in her expression. (James, *Complete Stories*, p. 526)

She's making him an offer. But the offer is framed and hedged by inanimate and perfected beauties (the clock, the china) and by her own infirmity (her wasted face), which moves her away from the sweat and blood of the living and toward the crystal and metal of the artifact (the white lustre of silver). She is assimilated to the inanimate, and all he can do, in spite of his conviction that she is right that there is a gift to give and receive (James makes this clear in the lines immediately following those quoted), is wait, with the outcome signalled by his inability to do anything else (he only waited). They continue to wait, silently, expectantly, but,

The end, none the less, was that what he had expected failed to sound. Something else took place instead, which seemed to consist at first in the mere closing of her eyes. She gave way at the same instant to a slow, fine shudder, and though he remained staring—though he stared, in fact, but the harder—she turned off and regained her chair. It was the end of what she had been intending, but it left him thinking only of that. (James, *Complete Stories*, p. 527)

The gift cannot, now, be given or received. He still doesn't know what it was, this ungiven gift, though she, and the reader, by now see it clearly.

She tells him no more, and a page or two later she dies. The beast has sprung and wreaked its havoc on his life, but he is still unsure what that havoc, really, has been. Was it just that his friend, May, has died before him? That doesn't seem enough, he thinks; it doesn't seem adequate to his certainty, shared by her, that his life would be up-turned by the beast, and not in a way that he would like.

John grieves May's death the more intensely because he has no public position as bereaved. He can't mourn her publicly as a husband or a brother or a father might, and so his grief remains private. He travels to forget her and his grief for her, but he fails in both. And, worse perhaps, his conviction that he is no longer marked for disaster because the beast in the jungle has now done its work—he believes what she told him about this—empties his life of significance. He wanders in a wasteland, and when he returns, after some time, to En-gland, he visits her grave. While there, he sees true and deep grief dis-played by another man at a nearby grave. This, at last, shows him what his disaster has been. He has never loved her for herself, and he has never seen and acknowledged her as what she was to him, which was a lover, a true intimate, one who was prepared to offer herself to him fully, acknowledging each of them as what they were. Instead, he has treated her as useful to himself, his companion in bearing his secret who would not, however, be allowed to disturb or alter his life or any of its fundamentals. He has been blind, cold, and egotistical, living outside the sphere of gift and acknowledgment and inside the walled city of dead, ordered beauty. And now it is too late for any-thing to be otherwise. Now all he can do is grieve his loss—of her, of a life that was not, and of his capacity to do anything about any of it. These losses are what the jungle beast has inflicted and they are all the more damaging because they are self-inflicted. John is the beast he was waiting for, and the leap, the claws, and the evisceration are all his own.

At the story's end he feels intense pain as he realizes the truth of things, and it is pain that although "belated and bitter, had some-thing of the truth of life." But he can't bear even that lively bitterness, and he turns from it toward May's tomb, filling his eyes with death. At that point, his lament loses any tincture of regret, any tincture of otherwiseness. The dreadfulness of what has happened is now the only thing for him, which means that grief is the only thing for him. His regret has become remorse, of a kind and intensity not unlike that depicted by Dickinson. What James adds to Dickinson, at least by suggestion, is that regret, and thereby also remorse, can be future-directed. John knows in advance that the beast will, in the future, have sprung, and he knows this long before he knows what that spring will do; he also regrets, anticipatorily, that future state of affairs. He knows, too, by the time he has understood what the beast was and what it has done, that he will grieve its spring, which was self-caused, until the end of his life, and he will, at the end of that life, be remorseful at having spent its bulk in culpable ignorance and its latter part in incurable remorse. At this point, again as with Dickinson, remorse has dissolved into lament; John has left otherwiseness behind and is now immured in grief.

There are in James's story — and in this it differs from Dickinson's poem — moments of opening into otherwise-thought, moments, that is, in which there's not only cureless remorse but also the possibility of action that would transfigure the past and refigure (newly configure) the future. If John had responded to May's move toward him at the story's crux, if he'd been able to acknowledge her as a person rather than a companion in connoisseurial acquisition (those morsels of rosy Dresden), they might have become lovers even at that late stage — and then the wasted years would have become not a wasteland but a courtship, overextended perhaps, but still a courtship. A strength of James's story is that it at once provides, in its central conceit, a strong depiction of failure's inevitability (John is convinced that the beast will leap no matter what he does), a strong depiction of its non-inevitability (neither Bartram nor the reader is convinced that the leap must occur), and the excellent suggestion, deep in the story's bowels, that the beast's pounce is to be found at least as much in John's settled conviction that it will pounce as it is in his failure to acknowledge what Bartram is to him. Without that connection, penitence and contrition might have been possible. With it, they are not; the past yields only Dickinsonian remorse and the future becomes a place where there can only be more of the same.

"Remorse" isn't the only word you might use for the attitude James and Dickinson depict. But it's a good one. Its etymology suggests a gnawing pain, a constant background agony that no diversion can completely obscure. When the rat is stripping the flesh from your bones or the cancer-crab is ravaging your organs from the inside, or when the torturer is separating your nails from your toes, the pleasures of the world, the flesh, and the devil won't distract you much. It may seem overheated to liken the presence to you of your past to these intensities of externally inflicted pain. But it really isn't. The endless loop that replays the things you did, the things that it seems, to you, that you ought not to have done, can drive you mad; it can certainly rival repetitive and intense physical pains—not with immediate agony but with the fillip of knowledge that you have done and are doing this to yourself. The rat and the crab and the torturer, you can tell yourself, are other than you, mere external agents. Their work isn't yours, whereas what you feel remorse for is yours, as is the remorse you feel. You did it and you can't undo it; those facts bite in a way and with an intensity that no externally effected pains can match. Further, in remorse's more extreme cases, a key ingredient to the agonizingly regrettable presence of your past is the sense that this agony will never go away. The remorseful are like Lady Macbeth in finding it impossible to wash themselves clean of their past misdeeds; if the blood shed at Lady Macbeth's instigation can't be washed away even by all the water of the sea, the laments of the remorseful are equally incapable of cleansing their past sins. Whence remorse as the mordance, the rat bite. Whence Dickinson's characterization of it as hell's adequate. And whence James's depiction of it as useless in salving the self-inflicted wounds of the beast in the jungle.

Isn't it then better to be the kind of person who doesn't suffer remorse? If there really is no exit from that circle of hell, and if nothing about the past can be changed by having remorse for one's contributions to its horrors, then surely one ought to cultivate blindness to those contributions or at least detachment from the sense of responsibility from them. In that way at least one of the things the remorseful suffer for and lament—the sense that I did this, that I am its agent— might be removed. Dickinson's remorse and James's beast would seem pointless, and indulgence of them masochistic and self-dramatizing.

Perhaps. It's certainly the case that not everyone is subject to remorse's mordancy, whether because of a lack of a sense of the wrongness of anything they've done (the cat feels no remorse for the pains it's inflicted on the mouse), or because of a preference not to think about their own past wrongs (that preference can be cultivated), or because of a weak identification (or even a complete lack of identification) with their own pasts (that too can be cultivated, and in extreme cases can yield a break in one's sense of continuity with one's past). It's also true that a clinician's response to a diagnosis of unbearable remorse might reasonably be a prescription that moves the sufferer in one or more of these directions. But blindness, even if it removes the pain of seeing horrors, remains a lack; a detachment from one's own past simpliciter, or from any sense of responsibility for it, is detachment from a real relation. And so a clinical recommendation of these responses to remorse is best understood, if it's defensible at all, as a needs-must response like a surgeon's amputation of a gangrenous limb in order to save a patient's life. If there is a better way than blindness to respond to remorse, it should be followed. And there is.

CHAPTER SIX

Contrition

REMORSE'S MORDANCY IS LAMENT-LACED PAIN. AS IS TYPICAL of intense pain (toothache, gallstones, childbirth), it's closed: those suffering it can see nothing beyond it. For them, it has no outside. They—we—can and do wish otherwise both the rat-gnawing pain and the past actions in whose presence the pain consists. But when we are in the grip of remorse, we cannot by our own effort and intention loosen that grip. It is, for the time being, all there is for us. We are George Orwell's Winston in Room 101, thronged by the spectres of our past sins. There's no exit from that room.

Sometimes though, unpredictably, remorse gets broken open, ground down, rubbed out, sandpapered smooth, exhausted. Those locutions are all possible renderings of the Latin verb *conterere*, whose participle is *contritus*, whence the English adjective "contrite" and the noun "contrition." Contrition is an activity: it rubs away at whatever it's directed at, sandpapers it smooth, thins it out, and, sometimes, breaks it open. Triteness—a word derived from the same root as contrition—does the same thing to language; when we say of an expression or a sentiment that it's trite (your love is like a red, red rose), we connote, knowingly or not, the thought that the expression has been rubbed smooth, worn out by use. It's lost its grip, the purchase it once had, and now it slides, frictionless and barely noticeable, across the surface of our speech and thought. Once, perhaps, when Burns used it, it was rough and startling: perhaps it then brought those who heard and read it up short, arresting them as sharply and irresistibly as Dickinson's characterization of remorse as the adequate of hell now does. But no longer. Use has made it trite, a cliché. Contrition can do the same to the rat bite of remorse. It can make mordancy trite.

It's not that contrition is an inevitable concomitant of remorse. Remorse doesn't wear itself out or smooth itself down or break itself open; its ordinary end isn't triteness but constant, unbearable intensity. It burnishes itself bright every morning. Here there's a disanalogy with what use does to language. There, triteness follows ineluctably upon repetition. Not so with remorse. It can remain what it is forever, world without end. The instrument of contrition—the thing that contrition is—affects its object, which in this case is remorse's mordancy, differently than repetition affects language. Contrition introduces into remorse something alien and external to it—namely, a grief that doesn't have to do with the suffering of the remorseful one but is instead directed, principally or exclusively, at the wrongness of what was done, which is to say at the damage done by infliction, whether that damage was inflicted upon living or inanimate things, people or other animals, a tree or the world. If I'm remorseful at my own past wastefulness of food, let's say, then I'll be concerned now with the pain caused to me by the active memorial presence of those damage-producing acts—of the times when I've thrown food away rather than storing it for later; of the times when I've caused pain to others by unnecessarily speaking harsh rather than comfortable words; of my betrayals and violence and lies. That pain, the mordancy, is mine, and suffering it is what gives remorse its characteristic, closed-in feel. In its grip, I attend only to myself; by contrast, the grief of contrition is directed outside myself, at the damage done, and in being so directed it wears down and breaks open the closed horizon of remorse. In both remorse and contrition I would it were otherwise, but in the former what I wish otherwise is some feature of myself, and in contrition what I wish otherwise is some feature of the world. In remorse, I want my pain to go away; in contrition, I begin to want the world's damage to be redressed. For the contrite, the self recedes and the world opens before their gaze in its damaged glory. Contrition redirects the gaze—or, better, in the case of the otherwiseness proper to it, contrition is just a redirection of the gaze—from one's own apparently irremediable sufferings to the damage done to people and things other than oneself.

JANE AUSTEN'S *EMMA*, WRITTEN IN 1814–1815 AND THE LAST OF her works to be published in her lifetime, isn't centrally about regret in any of its varieties, but regret, remorse, contrition, and repentance, bound together and separated in various ways, are nevertheless frequent presences in the story. That is because the novel is centrally about the moral formation of an intelligent, witty, arrogant, and self-satisfied young woman, Emma Woodhouse, and that formation involves Emma developing the capacity to see and acknowledge some of her faults. Emma's wit and intelligence are evident and pleasing to herself, and so are the dullness and foolishness of most of those with whom she interacts. She feels herself licensed thereby, as Austen depicts her, to manipulate and sometimes to insult others, confident in the rightness of her judgments and the usefulness of her judgments to those she manipulates. She's confident, too, that those she insults are often too stupid to see that she's doing so. Emma is young, in her early twenties, which means, for Austen's time and place, ripe for marriage, perhaps even overripe. Gradually, over the course of the novel, she learns, with the help of others and by the force of circumstance, that her wit, however real, is not sufficiently coupled with moral intelligence and that the recipients of her insults can be hurt by them even when they cannot quite understand her or, understanding, cannot quite say that they have been insulted.

Emma's treatment of Hetty Bates can serve as an emblematic instance. Hetty is the poor, middle-aged (perhaps in her forties), unmarried daughter of a long-deceased vicar of the village in which the novel's action takes place. Her principal task is the care of her old and infirm mother, and she is tolerated, but not loved, by those around her. She is gossipy, trivial, and unintelligent. Emma sees all that clearly, and readers of *Emma* see it through her eyes while also being shown by Austen that what Emma sees is not the whole truth. Bates is content, even happy, in a situation that would be unendurable for Emma; she cares for her mother with devotion, and is grateful for her inclusion in social events — dinners, dances, excursions — by her social and financial betters, whom she acknowledges to be such.

One day there's an excursion to Box Hill, a place of local beauty. Hetty is included in the party; Emma is there too, as are all those of any social significance in the neighborhood. It's intended as a lively summer event, something out of the ordinary run. But conversation languishes; it's a hot day and several of the participants are out of sorts. Emma, through Frank Churchill, one of her mouthpieces, tries to enliven things by asking each member of the party to provide "either one thing very clever, be it prose or verse, original or repeated — or two things moderately clever — or three things very dull indeed, and she engages to laugh heartily at them all." Hetty is the first to respond. She says that this will be no difficulty for her because she will be sure to "say three dull things as soon as ever I open my mouth." Emma responds at once: "Ah! ma'am, but there may be a difficulty. Pardon me — but you will be limited as to number — only three at once" (*Emma*, vol. 3, ch. 7, p. 347). Hetty understands at once what's meant, and is hurt.

Later, George Knightley, Emma's suitor though not at this stage of the novel declared as such, upbraids Emma for needless cruelty to someone who lacks her advantages of beauty, wit, money, and social standing. Emma, he says, should have shown compassion to Hetty and was instead insolent and unfeeling. She, reluctantly, sees that what George says is true and feels remorse of a Dickinsonian kind:

> Never had she felt so agitated, mortified, grieved, at any circumstance in her life. She was most forcibly struck. The truth of his representation there was no denying. She felt it at her heart. How could she have been so brutal, so cruel to Miss Bates. . . . Time did not compose her. As she reflected more, she seemed to feel it more. (*Emma*, vol. 3, ch. 7, p. 352)

This is exactly "A Presence of Departed Acts — / At window — and at Door" as Dickinson describes, and it is as painful for Emma as the departed acts are for the remorseful in Dickinson's poem.

The cause of Emma's remorse is, or might seem, trivial: a few cutting words spoken without much thought. The display of wit by the witty is often, as in Emma's case, a sufficiently ingrained habit that it's done without attention to or interest in the pain it might cause. Emma's verbal cleverness seems fluently inevitable, as greenness is for an emerald. But Austen's language about it is strong, and it shows Emma's behavior as morally serious and capable of correction. Both George and Emma herself are depicted as taking it so, and readers are moved to do so as well. What Emma has said to Hetty is insolent, unfeeling, and brutal. She has wounded someone who lacks the capacity or power to respond in kind, as an equal, and she has thereby abused both her power and the person she's insulted. Emma, not long after she's spoken in this way to Hetty, arrives at clarity about what she's done and is agonized by it. But, unlike Dickinson's remorse, which proposes no cure and can, in principle, find none, Emma sees a cure, or if not a cure then at least a remedy, for herself: "In the warmth of true contrition, she [Emma] would call upon her [Hetty] the very next morning, and it should be the beginning, on her side, of a regular, equal, kindly intercourse" (*Emma*, vol. 3, ch. 7, p. 353). Emma pays the planned visit, congratulating herself on her righteousness as she does and hoping that George will see her displaying it and will think better of her than he seems to her to have done until this point in the novel. This gives the reader pause. Emma may have been convicted by George and may have come to share his judgment of her conduct, but that doesn't much reduce her self-centeredness: her promise to herself that she will amend her relations with Hetty doesn't in the least prevent her from approving her own virtues and hoping to impress someone whose opinion she values. Austen rarely depicts unmixed motives, and she certainly refrains from doing so here. On the morning after the Box Hill outing, Emma does go to visit Hetty, but she neither apologizes for nor mentions her conduct on the previous day. Hetty makes few appearances in the remainder of the novel, and there is therefore no thick description of a healing of relations between her and Emma. There is, however, a detailed depiction of Emma's remorse for and repentance of her meddling with her protégé Harriet Smith's marriage plans, and of her realization of her blindness about George's character and intentions.

Each of these changes involves, first, clarity of vision on Emma's part about the wrongs she's done in the past; then contrition for those wrongs; and, last, actions intended to redress the wrongs done, to the extent possible. In the case of matchmaking and match-unmaking for Harriet, Emma renounces these interferences and blesses Harriet's marriage to a local farmer whom she'd previously dismissed as not good enough for her protégé and whose courting of Harriet she'd interfered with. And in the case of George, she accepts his offer while confessing her past faults to him, as he also does to her. Readers see Emma changed by her contrition and its consequent actions, changed, that is, in her understanding of and attitude toward her past (she now sees as wrong what had seemed to her either right or morally neutral) and in her capacity to act differently toward those she's wronged. If the burden of remorse as Dickinson and James depict it can be lifted, these, it appears, are the means.

Contrition and redress don't make the offenses of the past as if they'd never happened, but in reconfiguring Emma's attitude toward and understanding of them, as well as the mode of her future actions, the bite of remorse is made less painful. It's a weakness of *Emma*, perhaps, that there's no depiction in it of Emma's future relations with Hetty that are detailed enough to show their redemption. But that absence is also a strength. Emma's character is well-formed, with arrogance and contempt as central features of it, as they may also have been of Austen's character; there are few prose works in English—perhaps only Jonathan Swift's—so marked by these traits in their authorial voice. Features of that kind aren't quickly or easily changed, and Austen's sowing of seeds of doubt about whether Emma's contrition goes as deep as she thinks it has, and, therefore, about whether Emma's conduct toward Hetty includes the public acknowledgment of fault necessary for thoroughgoing amendment, shows a deep psychological realism. If there were redemption of the Emma-Hetty relationship, Emma's contrition for her brutality and her showing of kindness to Hetty would have been the principal means of it, which is also to say the principal means by which the teeth of Dickonsonian remorse can be eased from the flesh they bite. But arriving at contrition is hard, and arriving at the actions it suggests even harder; Emma, in *Emma*, has gone only partway, but there is somewhere for her to go, as there is not for John Marcher in Henry James's "The Beast in the Jungle."

EMMA'S CONTRITION ISN'T ENTAILED BY HER REMORSE. SHE MIGHT have seen the value and validity of George's analysis of her behavior toward Hetty, suffered because of it, and yet not turned her gaze toward Hetty's suffering. When she does that, and when she intends amendment of her conduct toward Hetty, and most especially when she begins to act on that intention (even if imperfectly and inadequately and with mixed and dubious motives), she exhibits exactly *animi dolor ac detestatio est de peccato commisso, cum propositio non peccandi de cetero* (sorrow at and detestation of sins committed, together with resolve not to sin further), which is the Council of Trent's definition of contrition. Among the causes of her contrition is George's catechizing: he instructs her in what she has done and thereby makes it possible for her to see something she hadn't seen before. That something—Hetty's suffering as a result of her, Emma's, thoughtless verbal violence—is the fact of damage, done not to herself but to someone else. Once she's seen that, the closedness of remorse can be broken open and Emma can be moved into the open, if rough, ground of loving action directed toward someone other than herself. That remains impossible for those caught in remorse. They, like most of us most of the time, are solipsists. They can be catechized out of their solipsism, but not easily and never finally; and even when the catechism is offered well and repeatedly—when the parent, over time, repeatedly tells and shows the small child that there are creatures in the world other than herself, and that they can suffer, and that she can hurt them—nothing is guaranteed. Solipsism remains the ordinary bedrock of our lives and when it's shattered, as it can be, there's always something odd, against the stream, about that happening. The same is true of altruism. The Catholic Church has recognized this oddity by saying of contrition that it's a supernatural gift. That is at least to say that it can't be bootstrapped and that no human action is sufficient condition for its occurrence.

Emma's contrition is directed at actions she's committed: her gaze has been turned by George toward what she had said to Hetty and, most importantly, toward Hetty herself as hearer of Emma's words. This situation is also one to which the Council of Trent's definition of contrition was intended to apply—that is, a situation in which you're contrite for what you've done in the past, and one in which your remorse for your own actions is redirected toward the effect of those past actions on others. That's very well: it's central to the ordinary understanding of contrition. But there's no reason to limit contrition (or remorse) to what you've done yourself. Even though it sounds odd on the face of it, you can be both remorseful and contrite for things you didn't do.

For example, it's an ordinary feature of life on this planet that there are periodic mass extinctions, events, or complexes of events in which a significant portion of species then inhabiting the earth is brought to an end. The proximate cause of these extinctions is always a change in the habitats or ecosystems that are necessary for the continued existence of some species or another. Imagine a species of lizard that can survive only where there is a mean temperature of at least eighteen degrees Celsius (sixty-four degrees Fahrenheit); imagine further that much of the planet has had, for some tens of millions of years, a mean temperature higher than that, which is good for these lizards; and then suppose that some event or other—it doesn't, for these purposes, matter what—suddenly, within a millennium or two, makes the planet such that nowhere on it does the mean temperature reach that level. That species of lizard will come to an end: it won't have time to evolve to meet the changes, and it won't be able to adjust to them in any other way. Habitat changes of this kind have been brought about in various ways (asteroid collision, alterations in planetary orbit, changes in atmospheric conditions, human agency, and so on), and there is often debate about how such distant causes work together and about what, in particular cases, they are. But in essentials, the picture is always the same: there is some more-or-less drastic and more-or-less short-term change in some ecosystem, and as a result, a species comes to an end.

In the case of species extinctions occurring before you, or any human, existed, it's clear that you did and can have done nothing to directly effect it. You're not related to the extinction of the dinosaurs as Austen's Emma is to Hetty or James's John is to May. You didn't extinguish them and there's nothing you can do to bring them back, Hollywood fantasies notwithstanding. It might seem, then, that while you might wish the dinosaur extinctions otherwise, you can't reasonably be remorseful about them or exhibit contrition for them. It certainly sounds odd in English to say that you can: if someone claimed to suffer Dickinsonian remorse for the extinction of the brontosaurus, most speakers of that language would be puzzled. To claim contrition for it would be more puzzling still. You can, at most, feel regret for that unpleasantness. So it seems.

And yet English and other natural languages do accommodate the thought that we can be remorseful for and contrite about things we didn't do. Consider, for example, the genocide wrought upon Native Americans by European settlers beginning in the fifteenth century. I wasn't alive; I didn't do it; I couldn't have done it. Further, I was born and grew up in a country other than the United States, and when I came to know about this genocide as an adolescent, by reading, I felt related to it no more intimately than I did to, say, the Punic Wars and the Taiping Rebellion. The history of the United States, like that of the Roman Republic, was the history of some other people. I had no affective relation to it. But then I moved to the United States, began a life there, and eventually, after fifteen years or so, as a man in midlife, became a citizen of it. And then my relation to the genocide in question changed, as it also did to much else in the history of my adopted country. I became more intimate with it and began to feel something like remorse and even something like contrition for it. English accommodates this: it's not a malformation to say that I'm regretful about, remorseful for, or contrite about the actions of my fellow citizens, past and present. They are, in some sense, my people, and I, therefore, am part of them. Something similar is true of the relations I have with those even closer to me: I've apologized for things my children have done, and I have felt implicated in things my siblings have done.

In these cases, at least two things are in play. One is solidarity: I have solidarity, to different degrees, with my family members and with my fellow citizens. I have more of it with my son than with any other man of the same age because I begot him and didn't (so far as I know) beget any of them; I have more of it with citizens of the United States than with citizens of, say, India, because I share citizenship with the former and not with the latter. Solidarity permits, and in some cases requires, remorse and contrition in some degree for the actions of those with whom one is in solidarity. There are questions of degree here: it's one thing to be contrite for the deliberate gift of smallpox-ridden blankets to those without immunity to the disease if I did it myself; it's another to be contrite for it if some American five generations back did it. But the difference is one of degree, not one of kind. Part of what it means to become a citizen or the member of a family is to take on solidarities that do, and should (as our ordinary patterns of speech and thought show us), yield these possibilities to us.

Another way to put the same point is to say that awareness of solidarity directs the gaze in particular ways. I look differently at the actions of my offspring than I do at actions of yours; I look differently at the actions of my fellow citizens than I do at actions of people with alien citizenship. So, very likely, do you. The texture of the difference is no doubt complex; the point of importance here is that there is one, and that it is entwined with how you look at others. The principal instrument of contrition, recall, is also a redirection of the gaze: that's how the gaze, closed by remorse upon yourself, is opened and redirected to the damage done to others. Similarly, contrition for what you didn't do is made possible by seeing those with whom you weren't in solidarity as those with whom, now, to some degree, you are.

A second thing, additional to solidarity, is an understanding of the kinds of relationships that obtain in the world. The sense of solidarity, while perhaps principally a matter of affect (I feel sufficiently intimate with this person or group that I experience remorse and/or contrition for what they have done), implies an understanding, also, of the scope of our responsibilities. To be contrite for what a fellow American has done suggests that agency and responsibility aren't only a matter of individual action—that it's possible in some cases for your actions also to be mine and for me, therefore, to be accountable for them. Most codes of law recognize this pattern of thought in some cases: when my proxy signs a contract, I am bound; when my minor child plays truant, I may be sanctioned; reparations for offenses committed by one generation may be demanded of its descendants; and so on. These kinds of cases, however, are exceptions to the ordinary legal rule that you are to be held responsible only for those things you do *in propria persona*—that is, with your own hands. But it is certainly possible to think differently about this by extending solidarity more or less radically, with knock-on effects on what it's reasonable to be remorseful about and contrite for.

One example of such thinking belongs to most forms of Christianity. The fundamental judgment here is that all human creatures are in deep solidarity with one another because we share a common nature and have a common ancestor. Our first parents—Eve, mother of all the living as scripture has it, and Adam—did some things that affect us all. They acted in such a way as to damage themselves and to transmit that damage to us. The paradigmatic instance of that damage is mortality. What they did made them subject to death and made each of us subject to it as well. We have solidarity with them in that, and we have solidarity with them, too, in that each of us replicates, in small or large ways, the pattern of self-damage (of sin) that they began. Their solidarity with us extends temporally downstream and ours with them extends temporally upstream. When we lament our sins, and (sometimes) are contrite for them, we lament and are contrite also for theirs. They, when they became aware of their sins as such and exhibited contrition for them (as, arguably, scripture shows them doing), were being contrite proleptically for ours, which have theirs as necessary (not, of course, sufficient) conditions. We are, all of us, what we are because they were what they were, and their being what they were is participant in what we now are. This pattern of thinking explains the ease with which Christians identify the worst of sinners as themselves and the worst of sins as essentially—structurally—similar to their own condition as sinners who perform lighter sins—if indeed they are lighter. Christian advocacy of love for enemies and prayer for enemies involves the thought, usually implicit, that I am (we all are) in solidarity with my enemies, and that their sins, no matter how heinous, are possibilities for us, too, because of that solidarity. We, as Christians, can therefore reasonably feel and exhibit contrition for any and every human sin (nonhuman sins, if there are any, provide a different kind of problem). Without some such judgment as this Christian one, that extension of remorse and contrition makes no sense.

Christians, to the extent that we participate in this understanding of solidarity together with the extension of contrition it makes possible (many of the baptized don't participate in it much), have typically learned to do so by way of a broadly narrative catechesis. We've heard the story, in scriptural and homiletical forms, and have taken part in liturgical re-presentations of it, endlessly (cyclically, repeatedly) performed. So catechized, it's possible to be contrite for what Judas or Genghis Khan or Stalin has done: to show, to say, and perhaps also to feel that what they did is something to feel sorrow for and detestation of, as the Council of Trent has it, and to resolve not to do more of. Their sins, and yours and mine, are all alike in having roots in, together with exuberant growth from, the sin of Eve and Adam. Whenever you sin, Eve and Adam act in you, and your action is also theirs; your action and theirs are not in competition—that it's theirs doesn't mean it's not yours, and that it's yours doesn't mean it's not also theirs. This version of noncompetitive agency is the negative image of the version that, according to the better versions of Christian theology, relates your good actions to those of the triune LORD whom Christians worship. That LORD's preveniently good actions are the condition of the possibility of yours, and when you act well you do so only as—definitionally, exactly as—a proxy participant in the LORD's gift. So also, by remote analogy, for Eve-Adam's sin and yours. Your Christian participation in the good actions of the community (also a communion) of the saints means that you can rejoice in and at the goods they perform, and you can rejoice in and at yourself as proxy participant in those goods. So also for your remorse for and contrition at the sins of others.

That is the structure of Christian thought and practice on these matters. It is for most, baptized and not, counterintuitive and shocking. And it is moderated and constrained by Christianity as lived, as it must be. The moderation is given by acknowledging the fundamental and universal solidarity of all in sin, and therefore the limitlessness of remorse and contrition, and then by observing that contrition's redirection of the gaze is supposed to usher in action (as it did, however half-heartedly, for Austen's Emma) that, where possible and to the extent possible, redresses the damage done, and that address is always particular and local. You and I can't provide redress to the victims of the Shoah, any more than we can to those who suffered and died in the Taiping Rebellion or the Punic Wars. We can, perhaps, to some small extent, do that for persons whose flesh and soul we've directly damaged. If I've robbed you, slandered you, tortured you, or defrauded you, and if I'm not only remorseful but also contrite, then I may be able to do something of what's necessary to make good the damage. Not easily, not often, and never completely but somewhat, and on occasion. And so the confessor who hears you begin to narrate your contrition for the violence of all humanity will stop you and ask you to talk about what you've done, not about what everyone has done. That won't, ideally, be because he's rejecting the Christian structure of thought just described; he won't be denying your solidarity with the sins of Eve-Adam and thus with those of all humanity. Rather, it'll be because, again ideally, he's aware of finitude and of the need to get you to act. For those purposes, a narrow focus on contrition for what you've done in thought and word and wordless physical action is the right thing.

What, then, of Christian contrition for the extinction of the dinosaurs? This, following the ordinary chronology, doesn't and can't involve any human agency — not yours, and not that of Eve-Adam. That's because there were no humans extant when the last of the dinosaurs died. That, anyway, is what the palaeontologists say, and it is concordant with one aspect of the scriptural narrative, according to which the LORD's creation of humans follows that of other animate creatures. How, then, from a Christian point of view, is it possible to hold the claim that sin is a necessary condition for death (no sin, no death, and that includes the deaths of nonhuman creatures as well as those of humans) together with the claim that death precedes humans? The ordinary solution is simple enough. It is to say that not all sin is human: angels too are capable of it, and it was angelic sin, prior to the creation of humans, that damaged the cosmos so that death could enter it. Human sin, on this view, reflects and recapitulates angelic sin, sharing in its structure. This in turn means that humans came into existence in an already damaged cosmos, an already blood-soaked slaughterhouse. The extinction of the dinosaurs belongs here, as an instance of the damage unleashed by angelic sin. There are, for Christian theologians, difficulties with and disputes about this account. I won't pause to engage with or expound on them, other than to say that it is on its face consistent with the empirical observations of those whose business it is to study and interpret the material remains of creatures who have lived on this planet, and that it is, in outline (though always with dispute about details), the standard pre-Reformation Christian account. It provides, too, resources for considering the nature of our—your and my—possible contrition for events such as the extinction of the dinosaurs.

Contrition has at its heart the turn of the gaze toward the damage done. That turning may produce *animi dolor*, sadness whose principal object is that damage rather than the condition of the one considering it. It may also produce, or at least contribute to producing, a resolution not to perform acts that result in damage of this kind. All this is possible for you even if not only did you not yourself contribute in any direct way to the state of affairs you're contrite for but you are also not a creature of the same kind as those who did. In the Christian case, you have solidarity with the angels too. It isn't a solidarity of creaturely kind, but it is a solidarity in sin. You, like them, are capable of sin; you, like some among them (Christian speculative theology exempts some among the angels not only from sin but also from its possibility), are a sinner; and all sin has essentially the same structure, so when you sin you do the same kind of thing the angels did when they fell and thereby introduced death into the world. It is that solidarity that makes possible and gives form to the contrition you can feel for the extinction of the dinosaurs. If you are contrite, as a Christian, in this way, it's likely because you've been catechized by some version of the account just given, and you have had the range of your vision extended thereby. The catechizing will have done for you what George's words did for Emma: it will have made it possible for you to extend the scope of your understanding of what you're complicit in producing.

Christian commitments, however, aren't the only ones capable of motivating such an extension of the sense of solidarity, together with a concomitant extension in contrition. Scholastic Indian Buddhism has conceptual resources for this that are in most ways more radical and thoroughgoing than anything in Christianity. A Sanskrit tag indicates the heart of the matter: *svaparātmasamatā*: the sameness—identity—of your—one's own—self with that of others. There is, according to the grammar of Buddhist thought on this matter, not merely a sameness of kind between you and others with selves; there is also nothing other than the obsessively ornamenting fictive proclivities of the mind to differentiate you from them—the tendency, that is, habitual and apparently ineradicable, to take a particular set of causes and effects to yield a substantive something called a self, and to think that you have yours and I have mine, and that I have interests in mine that I don't have in yours. There is, on this view, no subsistent you different from a subsistent me, and there are in general no unitary and enduring subjects of experience different from one another in any ontologically or morally significant sense. The thought that my sufferings are distinct from yours exactly in being mine and not yours is, on this view, a mistake, and a damaging one. The principal damage it provokes is that those who make it are very likely, as a result of making it, to be more concerned about their own sufferings than about those of others and to act in accord with that concern. Their compassion will have its scope radically restricted by this mistake. By contrast, those who cultivate (cultivation requires, as in the Christian case, attentiveness to instruction and the establishment of new habits) the sense that they don't own their sufferings, and that theirs are as much yours as yours are theirs (this is a key part of what *svaparātmasamatā* means), will find the scope of their compassion extended, in the extreme case boundarylessly. They may then find it possible to act as Gautama Śākyamuni did in one of his previous lives when he dismembered his own body in order to alleviate the hunger of a starving tiger.

I'm making complicated ethical and metaphysical matters simple here, perhaps too simple. But my purpose here isn't the exposition of standard-issue Indic Buddhist metaphysics; it's rather to make the single and simple point that there are ways other than the Christian one to extend the scope of contrition's anguish at, detestation of, and resolution to avoid further contributions to damage. Buddhas and bodhisattvas may reasonably be thought of by Christians as cultivating and exhibiting contrition for the world's damage by directing their gaze away from their own sufferings, including remorse for their own sins, and toward the damage done. This isn't, of course, the language of the account of these matters Buddhists would offer themselves; neither does it approach or attempt a Buddhist account of what it is that Christians do when they cultivate contrition, which is a subject I lack standing to treat.

Those who have radically individualist understandings of the world, unlike Buddhists and Christians, are not likely to be interested in extending contrition to damage they understand others to have inflicted. That is principally because they lack the conceptual resources to encourage the extension of a sense of solidarity in the (very different) ways that Buddhists and Christians can. It will seem odd to individualists, perhaps slightly crazy, to cultivate contrition for the extinction of the dinosaurs, or even to cultivate contrition for what members of your family, or your fellow citizens, have done or are doing. For them, contrition and its analogues ought to be provoked only by what you have yourself done, and the boundaries around that category are likely to be narrowly drawn. Individualists may, and do, lament states of affairs they've not contributed to themselves, but that is a very different matter.

Thomas Aquinas's treatment of contrition (*CONTRITIO*) illuminates, while also obscuring, the place the word has in Christianity's grammar. In his *Summa Contra Gentiles*, composed in the thirteenth century, his discussion of it occurs as part of his analysis of the sacrament of penance (it's to be found in the seventy-second chapter of the fourth book). He begins by noting, unimpeachably, that post-baptismal sin is possible for Christians notwithstanding the grace received in that sacrament. We do not, by virtue of baptism and the other sacraments, enter a condition in which we always know what is good and want what is good; our intellect and will remain mutable, which is to say that they can and do turn away from what is good, and sin is just such a turning away. But such post-baptismal sin is remediable, paradigmatically, by the sacrament of penance (*sacramentum poenitentiae*). On this Thomas quotes approvingly, among many other scriptural texts, Jeremiah 3:1, which, in the version he reads, has the LORD addressing Israel as one who has fornicated with many lovers but who nonetheless should return to the LORD's embraces. Return must therefore be possible, even after fornication. "From all these [texts], it's clear that if the faithful should lapse after [receiving] grace, a return to health is open to them."

Yes. Fair enough. What then is that return? It's a kind of spiritual cleansing (*spiritualis sanatio*), which is to say a remedy that purges sinners of their sins and restores them to the healthy condition from which their sins had removed them. Thomas's imagery is here medicinal from top to bottom: sin damages our health; the sacrament of penance, which is the remedy, removes the damage; and we are thus made healthy again. "The spiritual cure that belongs to [the sacrament of penance] wouldn't be complete unless people were lifted out from under (*sublevaretur*) all the damage (*detrimentum*) done to them by sin." And the first instrument for this lifting out from under is contrition, whose definition (*ratio*) is "grief for the sin committed and resolve not to commit it again." That mixture of grief and resolution, Thomas says, has the immediate effect of redirecting (*convertere*) the sinner's gaze to the LORD and turning it away from (*avertere*) the sinner's sin. And that turning exactly is spiritual health (*salus spiritualis*), which is the remedy for the problem.

There's an etymological point to be made here. *Peccatum*, sin, for Thomas, produces (or sometimes just is) a *detrimentum*, which I've translated as "damage," and *contritio* is the means by which the weight or burden of that damage is lifted from the sinner. *Contritio* and *detrimentum* are derived from the same root, and *conterere* (whence *contritio*) and *deterere* (whence *detrimentum*) have roughly the same meaning in Latin—that is, to rub or grind smooth, to remove (something) by friction. "Damage," then, is one reasonable rendering of *detrimentum*, so long as what's rubbed or smoothed away is a good thing, for then something good is lost, which is just what damage is. Contrition, though, indicates the same kind of smoothing/rubbing action, but only in a context where damage has already been brought about: it removes damage by smoothing something bad away, just as detriment produces (or just is) damage by smoothing something good away. There's a double negation at play here. Sin/damage (*peccatum/ detrimentum*) is parasitic upon goodness as sickness is parasitic upon health; all sin does is remove goodness, sandpapering it down and roughing it up. Sin can bring nothing into being because it has no independent existence. What it can do, and all it can do, is damage what there is by grinding it away. And the removal of damage must be done in an appropriately similar way. It isn't that damage is there to be attacked and removed; it's rather that the now-roughened surface of the mirror, abraded by accident and no longer capable of reflecting accurately what's before it, must be repolished, the abrasions ground away and the smoothness restored. That's what contrition is and does.

There's no evidence that Thomas has this etymological connection between *contritio* and *detrimentum* in mind. But emphasizing it, together with its grammatical implications for well-formed Christian talk, does show something about the structure of his analysis of *contritio*. Its sadness and resolution are restorative only (but importantly). They don't bring anything new into being—they restore what was there by removing adventitious damage, and what was there was *salus* (health). If contrition makes sin trite, it does that by removing sin's accidental grip on health, which is the only thing there really is.

CHAPTER SEVEN

Confession

EVERY UTTERANCE DOES SOMETHING TO THE UTTERER AND TO the world. At a minimum, when you say something—the weather's fine today, I'm worried that I might lose my job, the United States is a dysfunctional democracy, last night I slept unusually badly—you become what you weren't before, which is someone who's now said what you said. Correspondingly, the world becomes a world in which you've now said what you said. Those are novelties, even if uninteresting ones. Sometimes, though, an utterance does more: it at once binds together and mutually transforms the utterer and the object or addressee of the utterance. When I make a promise, or sign my name to a contract, or confess my faith in the LORD before the LORD's face, I do something with words that binds me, and in some cases also binds the one to whom I say (or write) the words. A contract between us, sealed with words, binds in both directions, as, though differently, does a promise. It's not that the bonds created in these ways can't be broken; obviously, they can. But even when they are, there's something, word-made, that needs to have effort directed at it sufficient to break it. When the LORD says *fiat lux*, that's the same as light's coming to be; there's no gap between the word and the deed because—for the LORD—the word is the deed. To speak is to make. It's not ordinarily so for us but sometimes we can, verbally, approach that degree of creative power. "I love you" isn't only, or even principally, a description of how I feel about you, it's an instance of that feeling-attitude, performing what it represents as the sacraments also do. The same is true of "I hate you"—that form of words is a blow, as the other is a caress.

"Avowal" is a good enough word for these peculiar utterances. The word contains the thought and sound of the vow, a weighty and performative promise that binds those who make it. To make an avowal is at least to take seriously the content of what you're saying (it's no light matter) and to understand yourself to be bound by and to what you're saying. Once you've avowed something, both you and the world are differently ordered: you've brought a new and weighty set of relations into being. That is a serious matter, and so avowals are taken seriously and typically flagged as serious. It's part of the ordinary texture of language—of all human natural languages, that is—to separate avowals syntactically and lexically from quotidian and lightweight utterances by the use of special words and forms. It's also common to mark them with ritualized gestures and to give them solemnity by the place in which and the people before whom they're uttered. When I was married in a medium-sized English city in 1975, I went with my spouse-to-be and members of our respective families, dressed more formally and groomed with more care than usual, to a place set aside for the performance of civil marriages, there to repeat, after a man with particular, legally defined, powers in this sphere, words of high-formal diction, and afterward to sign my name on paper to a form of those same words. That was an avowal, and all the elements of its occurrence framed and indicated it as such. What I avowed then was (something like) lifelong love for, loyalty to, and support of my spouse, and in doing that I constituted, as she also did, a new set of rights and obligations between us of such weight that their lifting many years later in the process of civil divorce in another country required the help of lawyers and the expenditure of money and time. A similarly well-marked set of words was in play when, in 1994, I took on the rights and duties of citizenship in the USA; there, too, was an avowal, framed and ornamented by a high secular liturgy (a Marine color guard; a representative of the Daughters of the American Revolution; a federal judge, etc.), and it was clear in the very form of the words used ("I hereby renounce allegiance to all foreign powers . . ." — consider that "hereby") that those words, and I in uttering them, were doing something, performing something, unusual and significant and transformative.

On this understanding of what it is to confess, I confess that the English have not infrequently shown genocidal tendencies toward the Irish. . . . I confess that from time to time I've offended against the strict requirement to tell the truth. . . . I confess that humans are contributing to the devastation of the planet's ecosystems. . . . I confess that I've never managed to finish Robert Musil's *Der Mann ohne Eigenschaften* or William Gass's *The Tunnel*, and so on. Confession, understood as the act of confessing, is intimate, therefore, with lament and remorse and contrition, sharing with them, to some or another degree, the thought, "I would it were otherwise." It differs from them in being necessarily public: they can remain inward, and most often do. The rat bite of remorse is typically a matter of feeling rather than expression; it can remain unexpressed (perhaps it most often does), and when it is expressed or delineated, the act of showing it is one of confession rather than one of remorse. Remorse is typically identified in its portrayals exactly as something that should be otherwise. It is, in that way, an object of confession. Contrition is closer to confession than are lament and remorse, but even it can be felt without being confessed.

In English, and in Christian theology, the verb "to confess" isn't used only for things you would rather not have done. You can confess Christ, or your love for the LORD, or your desire and affection for another human being, or your delight in the music of Mozart, or your American citizenship, without suggesting thereby that you regret any of these things. There is, in Christian talk, confession of praise and of faith as well as of sin, and a similar range of uses of the word is found, though more diffusely, in secular English as well. But here I'll use "confession" to indicate regretful avowals, avowals of states of affairs contritely wished otherwise by the one avowing.

All confessions are fictive in the sense that they're formed by artifice. They belong to the sphere of what's indicated, in Latin and English, as the carefully fashioned (from *fingere*) and elegantly made. They're prepared and polished and worked over as is the text of a novel, or a poem, or the polished silver of the chalice into which wine is poured for consecration. They're the place, the word-chalice, for the contrite identification of what ought to be otherwise, and just as the wine of the crucified one's blood is poured and given and received with precise and structured care, without spontaneity or naturalness (the crucifixion is the antithesis of a natural event, as are the vessels for the containment and sharing of what's been crucified, and as is the liturgy in which the crucified one is celebrated most intimately), so the matter of a confession is spoken and communicated and received with just such fictive care.

Confessions have, that is to say, a form, and it's the form of a fiction. This doesn't mean they aren't true, even though that has come to be one of the overtones of "fiction." It means that they're prepared and worked over, that they belong to a genre, and that they have their place in the sacramental economy as a pivotal moment in the identification and transfiguration of what isn't the way it's supposed to be. There's a rough but not useless analogy between the words of a confession and the words of institution: the former show, in public and by way of words, what becomes of damage by speaking of it as such with contrition (that is, transfiguration and release); the latter show, in public and by way of words, what becomes of bread and wine by speaking its participation in the flesh and blood of Jesus (that is, transubstantiation and healing). What makes a confession true, though fictional, is double: it should, in identifying states of affairs that ought to be otherwise, do so rightly; and it should be accompanied by contrition, a sense that those states of affairs are detestable, vacantly horrifying, and therefore lamentable. When those conditions are met, confessions are made.

IF CONFESSION IS UNDERSTOOD AS A PARTICULAR KIND OF AVOWAL, it must bring something about. What is that? What do contrite avowals perform and effect that contrition by itself (in this like its close cousins, remorse and lament) can't? Since the difference between contrition and confession is utterance, the answer to this question must have to do with utterance: what does contrite utterance do that contrition's sorrow and regret (*dolor ac detestatio*) don't? A first-blush answer might be that the confessional avowal's performativity is located in the fact that it communicates something to those who hear it—after all, utterances communicate while attitudes don't, or at any rate they don't do so in the same way. But there are good reasons for thinking that this commonsense answer isn't the right one, or at least doesn't suffice.

Augustine (among the most subtle theorizers and users of *confessio* and its cognates in the Christian archive and the first in that archive, and perhaps anywhere, to compose a work with that title) begins to show why and to indicate where a better answer might be found. At the beginning of the fifth book of his *Confessions* he writes:

> Accept the sacrifices of my confessions from my tongue's hand, which you created and enlivened so that it might confess your name. Also, heal all my bones so that they might say, "LORD, who is like you?". For those who confess to you don't teach you what's going on inside them. That's because neither does a closed heart shut out your gaze nor human hardness repel your touch. Rather, you shatter that hardness when you like, whether mercifully or punitively, and there is no one who can hide from your heat. Instead, then, my soul should praise you so that it might love you, and should confess your mercies to you so that it might praise you . . . re-making and true strength are there. (Augustine, *Confessions*, 5.1.1)

Augustine is here explicit in his denial that confession to the LORD communicates anything. It can't do that because the LORD always already knows *quid in se agatur* (what's going on with you) inside and out, no matter how extensive and intensive your efforts might be to hide this or that. Confession does not, therefore, communicate about your actions, intentions, affects, desires, or what have you. But confession does something. The key sentence in specifying what it does is: "Instead, then, my soul should praise you so that it might love you, and should confess your mercies to you so that it might praise you." Grammatically, each half of the sentence says that

Augustine's soul—by which he means himself—ought do *x* so that it might do *y*. The verbs (*laudet . . . amet . . . confiteatur*) are in the subjunctive, which is a mood that indicates potential, whether weakly (can, may, might) or more strongly (ought, should, must). At one end of that spectrum the subjunctive shades toward the imperative and at the other it shades toward the indicative, and there are many stopping places in between. My rendering indicates a strongly subjunctive meaning for the first verb in each half of the sentence ("should praise" for *laudet*, "should confess" for *confiteatur*) and a weaker subjunctive meaning for the second verb in each ("might love" for *amet*, "might praise" for *laudet*). Other renderings are certainly possible, but this one focuses the reader's mind on the key point, which is that *x* is a necessary condition for *y*, so that if you want *y*, you ought to or must do *x*.

What, then, are *x* and *y*? There are three kinds of action indicated in the sentence: confession (*confiteri*), praise (*laudare*), and love (*amare*). Augustine's claim is that you need to confess if you're going to be able to praise, and that you need to praise if you're going to be able to love. And the object of all these activities is the LORD— indirect (*tibi*) in the case of confession, direct (*te*) in the case of praise and love. This pattern of thought shows what confession does: it removes an obstacle, or perhaps an agglomeration of obstacles, to intimacy with the LORD, and it locates these obstructions within the confessor. Confession does something to the confessor, not to the LORD.

It's a verbal performance that changes the performer, and it does so by re-making (*refectio*), as is written at the end of the quoted passage. That's a strong, indeed a radical, claim. The confession-praise-love sequence relates those who perform it to the LORD in such a way that they're newly made. Whatever the obstructions were that confession is the first step in removing, they must be weighty in order for this to be the result of removing them. The language Augustine uses here echoes that in Genesis, where *facere*, "to make," is used alongside *creare*, "to create," for what the LORD does in order to bring humans into being. That act—giving us being *ex nihilo*—is recapitulated by the sequence that begins with confession, and the

almost-unavoidable thought this suggests is that the obstructions removed by confession and so on are as nothing, turning those weighed
down by them away from what is—paradigmatically the LORD, the
one who is—and toward what is not the LORD, which is always and
exactly nothing. What confession does is serve as a necessary condition for the praise-love that, when given to the LORD, results in the
regifting to us of the being that made us in the first place, and that
makes it possible for us to confess and praise and love now. The agent
in all this, as Augustine sees it, is the LORD rather than us. What
we do when we confess, therefore, isn't done by us apart from the
LORD; it is, rather, what our agency looks like when it's rightly ordered, which is to say directed toward the LORD in harmony with
and in response to what the LORD has given. This is a point of great
importance for Augustine in his later polemic against what he took
to be Pelagius's views on these matters; in his best moments he sees
that what this must mean is that human and divine agency aren't
competitors—that when we act rightly the LORD also acts fully in
what we do, which is just what it means for us to act rightly. But
it would be a diversion from the question at hand to explore those
matters. That question at hand here is: how, exactly, does confession remove obstacles between us and the LORD in such a way as
to permit our remaking? In now providing a speculative answer to
this question, I leave behind explicit engagement with Augustine, although most of what follows is suggested to me by reading him and
is concordant with what he writes.

    We have a number of models for understanding how an avowal
works on and changes the one making it even when its content is already fully known to its recipient. Most of these models are legal-
performative: judges present at naturalization ceremonies already
know that those gathered there intend citizenship. Why else would
they be there? When the citizens-to-be raise their right hands and
swear the oath of allegiance the judges learn nothing new. But those
who say the words of the oath change their relation to the judge
before whom they say them, and through her to the USA, for whom
she, in the ceremony, stands proxy. Augustine would say: "My soul
should confess allegiance so that it might vote." This kind of example
is familiar enough.

There are also nonlegal and noninstitutional models of how a noncommunicative avowal can change someone making it, even when its content is already, and fully, known to its recipient. Consider the apology, certainly a kind of avowal. Imagine that I've done you some harm—I've slandered you, let's say, as you see it, making false claims about you to others in such a way that your reputation and prospects are damaged. Suppose, too, that we have a close mutual friend, and you learn from this friend that I've repented of my slander—I've come to see, the mutual friend tells you, that what I've been saying about you is false and that I assumed it to be true because of my ideological commitments and biases. I don't like you, the mutual friend tells you, because I don't like what I take you to stand for, and so I was pleased, eager even, to pass on a damaging rumor about you as truth without assessing it. You're convinced by our mutual friend; I have indeed, you've come to think, changed my mind and conduct. Your conviction of this is deepened when you hear me on a talk show repudiating my slander of you. Now, you can see, I've showed my repentance, and my penitence, to the world.

But something is still missing. I haven't avowed my penitence directly to you, the one I harmed by my slander. You're glad to know that I've stopped slandering and that I'm sorry I did it. But there remains, as you see it, a barrier between us. It's one thing for me to avow my mistake to others; it would be another for me to avow it to you. But then, one day, I do just that: I come to you, humbly apologize for the wrong I've done you, and ask whether there's anything further I can do to make good the damage. By that avowal, I've removed an obstacle between us. It's not that there's anything new I need tell you: you already know that I'm sorry, that I no longer take the slander to be true, and that I've stopped spreading it. What's changed isn't your knowledge of me—in this my confession to you is like Augustine's analysis of confession to the LORD—rather, it's the removal of an obstacle. My apologetic confession has removed whatever it was that stood in the way of forgiveness—your offer of it and my acceptance of it.

It's not so easy to say just what the obstacle was that my apology removed. Formally speaking, it was just the absence of a face-to-face apology. That way of putting it, though hardly illuminating at first blush, does indicate something important: apologies, like confessions to the LORD, don't remove something positive and real and responsive to heavy earthmoving machinery. They remove a refusal, which is absence rather than presence, silence rather than speech, denial rather than affirmation. If I can't bring myself to face you and apologize to you, it's because I'm looking somewhere else (at myself, usually) and can't bring myself to look at you. All that's needed is for me to turn my face toward yours and say the words that accompany such a turning. Then the obstacle is removed. Ordinarily it's enough in the person-to-person case, as in the penitent-before-the-LORD case, to make the turn and say the words from Luke 18:13, *propitius esto mihi peccatori* ("have mercy on me, a sinner"); specification of the sin in question may, but need not, be involved. There, Augustine would say, is remaking, which is a graceful move from the absence that was the refusal to confess toward the presence that is the confession. In avowing my sins to the LORD or to you, I make myself present as what I am, which is the foremost among sinners (1 Timothy 1:15).

CONFESSION AS RECOMMENDED AND PRACTISED IN THE LITURGIES of the Catholic Church is, for the most part, first-personal and in the singular. That is, those who confess, whether in a communal liturgy (Mass, some or another of the liturgies of the hours, a communal liturgy of penance) or to the ears of one priest within the celebration of the sacrament of penance, speak in their own voice and in the first person singular. For example, one formulaic introduction to the identification of a penitent's particular sins is: "I confess to Almighty God, to his Church, and to you, Father, that . . ." And the general confession in the introductory rites of the order of Mass begins: "I have greatly sinned, . . . in what I have done and in what I have failed to do. . . ." It's important, so the Church thinks, that you avow both that you've done what you ought not to have done and that you've not done what you ought to have done, and in that way you take responsibility for your sins and remove the obstacles that not avowing your responsibility would leave in place. You can confess generically ("I have greatly sinned, . . . in what I have done and in what I have failed to do") or specifically (I lied to her last Tuesday, stole from him three times this month, and harbored fantasies of revenge against them on at least three occasions since the beginning of the week). There are deformities proper to each mode, as well as advantages proper to each; which place on the spectrum is preferred depends on variables particular to individual situations. With respect to confession in the narrow sense—the confession of sin, that is—the Western churches emphasize the importance of both the general and the particular. General confessions occur, for example, in the order of Mass in two places: as an element of the *ritus initiales* preparatory to the liturgy of the word; and then as a thread in the *ritus communionis*, the Communion rite proper, evident in the Agnus Dei (*miserere nobis*) and most fully in the *non sum dignus* (*Domine, non sum dignus ut intres sub tectum meum* . . . ["O Lord, I am not worthy that you should enter under my roof . . ."]) immediately preceding the reception of the consecrated elements. There's nothing specific in these confessions: we, all of us, are sinners generically, committing grievous faults by omission and commission generically, and in need of mercy generically. Fault and damage are features of the human condition, as Christian doctrine affirms, and that state of affairs is what's dramatized in this aspect of liturgical confession.

There's also, however, the rite that constitutes the sacrament of penance, which places considerable emphasis upon the individual penitent's confession of particular sins. The priest is instructed at the appropriate place in the rite to help the penitent to make an integral confession, which means a spoken acknowledgment of as many particular sins as are remembered. Latin rite Catholics also have available to them various (optional) forms for examination of conscience as preparations for the rite proper, and these typically encourage those preparing to confess to ask questions of themselves whose answers could be quick, simple affirmatives or negatives, but which more naturally suggest a specific accounting. For instance: "Do you share your possessions with the less fortunate?" You could simply say yes or no, but the saying of either requires thought about how you do this, or don't, and occasions upon which you have, or haven't. Memory is the principal device, and activating it requires some introspection: "Last Thursday I was asked for money by a beggar, and I refused him even though I had money in my pocket." In either case, general or particular confession, what's required is an avowal, typically in speech but conceivably also, or instead, in other forms (writing, sign), of the fact of your sin and your contrition for it.

Specificity in confession comes in degrees. You can say, "I stole last week," or you can say, "Last Tuesday I took eighteen dollars from my mother's purse and spent it on Wild Turkey." You can say, "several times since my last confession I've imagined having sex with someone I'm not married to," or you can say exactly what the content, visual, tactile, olfactory, and so on, of those imaginations was. The greater the detail given, the more the introspective and memorial effort needed, and the greater, therefore, the fictionalization—the burnishing, ornamenting, and narrativizing—of what's confessed. Memorial introspection doesn't yield a three-dimensional sensorium in which your past replays itself before your present eyes (and ears, and . . .), so that you can then retell it to the one hearing your confession. It isn't possible to report on your past in that way; it isn't there for you to look at in anything like the way that would make that possible. You can only represent it, typically by way of dramatic stories, and for that you need imagination, verbal skill, fluency in the genre of the confession (internally differentiated and complex as that genre is), knowledge of what counts as confessable sin and what doesn't, and knowledge of the categories to which particular acts belong. Children in the Latin rite Catholic tradition are instructed in rudimentary forms of all this as they prepare for their first reconciliation at the age of seven or so.

Confessions toward the detailed end of the spectrum of specificity are more like short stories or poems or histories than like ships' logs or chronicles. Those latter confessions stay close to the ground and eschew as much as possible reference to cause and effect or to imponderables such as intentions, affections, entelechies, and patterns. Consider the difference between confessing what you did (I lied to him about my income) and confessing why you did it and what your motive signifies (I wanted to impress him, which is a besetting sin of mine; or, someone else was present whom I wanted to mislead in order to get her to do something that would harm her, and I wanted to do that because I hate her; or, what I said to him seemed true to me at the time because I've lied about my income so often that I no longer know what it is; etc.). The former is more like a log (sunrise 7:20 a.m.; wind nor'nor'west; no ships seen); the latter is more like a history. But even the former requires a good deal of interpretive and conceptual work. To say that you lied about your income requires some sense of what it is to lie, which is no simple matter (there's a flourishing theoretical literature on the question); and, perhaps, some sense of why lying is a confessable sin, again by no means a simple matter; and, of course, an understanding of what an income is, which, as all who fill out their tax returns know, is no simple matter. And if those are difficult, specification of cause and intention and pattern is vastly more so. Your intentions and desires are, as a matter of principle, neither transparent nor fully available to you; entire industries (advertising, political campaigns in democracies) are successfully predicated upon that assumption. There are many reasons for that lack of transparency and availability, not least among which is that everything you do is overdetermined with respect to cause and purpose to such an extent that you'd need to be Henry James or Marcel Proust to stand a chance of depicting even the main causal and purposive threads in the fabric of your actions, and whatever your novelistic or phenomenological skills might be, you've no chance at all of giving an exhaustive account of them. At one end of the confessional spectrum, then, is the finely wrought novel (your version of *The Golden Bowl*); at the other end of the spectrum is the simple log of actions with as much avoidance of specificity and talk of intention as possible (Monday, adultery; Tuesday, blasphemy; Wednesday, theft; etc.). The one type of confession seeks to depict the past in Proustian mode with the confessor as protagonist; the other type of confession aspires to be a record of external events without appeal to inner theater. And there is much in between.

There are several reasons why avowals that veer toward James are neither a good idea nor, usually, encouraged by the Church.

The first is their unreliability. As adumbrated in the preceding paragraph, novels and poems can be beautiful, and can be windows into the soul. But memoirs and autobiographies and other kinds of autofiction need as much imaginative artistry as do novels and poems, and that entails the likeness of those depicted in them to fictional characters.

The second is their superfluity. A good avowal, one that performs everything necessary for contritely regretful avowals, need do no more than say, first-personally, that the confessor has offended by commission and omission in particular ways (as liar, as thief, as luxurious glutton, as violent oppressor, by lust, by avarice, by fear, by hatred, as gossip) and with approximate frequency (hourly, daily, weekly, occasionally, rarely, once, sometimes, on nights when the moon is full). Specifying to whom these things were done, with what intentions, and with which particular movements of the body is unnecessary for the removal of obstacles between the confessor and the LORD. To offer such details to the LORD would be like explaining the physiological and neurological mechanisms by which the finger crooks in order to confess that you pulled the trigger. Confessing such particulars is an instance of the fallacy of misplaced concreteness, and it is ordinarily beyond your capacity in any case.

The third is their connection with egotism. You, like me, are not very interesting and very likely less interesting than you think. That is certainly the case with respect to contritely regretful avowals. At the level of the loggable action there aren't many kinds of sin, and yours aren't likely to have broken new ground or to be in any other way interesting. It's of the essence of sin not to be interesting because every particular sin is constituted, at its core, by the same gesture, which is the parasitic one of avoidance, the turn of the gaze from something toward nothing, and so your particular sins, whatever they are, will also not be generically interesting and will, in their particularity, be nothing more than repetitions of kinds of actions performed by millions before you and to be done again by millions after you. To depict your sins ornamentally, by placing them on the stage of your inner theater, inevitably fosters your sense of importance and uniqueness — the spotlight picks you out, and in its heat and light you strut and fret, even while avowing your strutting and fretting and thereby persuading yourself that you're not really strutting and fretting, which intensifies the strut and fret.

GEORGE HERBERT DIED OF CONSUMPTION IN MARCH 1633, NOT long before he would have been forty. At some time during the decade before that, he wrote a poem called "Confession" in five six-line stanzas (Herbert, *English Poems*, pp. 442–43). The first three stanzas treat grief and affliction. These are agonies we do our best to protect ourselves from. We construct hiding places, inventively and ingeniously, into which we hope affliction won't find a way: "within my heart I made / Closets; and in them many a chest; / And like a master in my trade, / In those chests, boxes. . . ." But we fail in this because the LORD's afflictions, those that come because of sin and because of the Fall of the world, "are too subtill for the subt'llest hearts," and they are that because they are from the LORD and there's no way at all to guard oneself from the LORD: "No smith can make such locks, but they have keyes." No escape, then: sin is followed inevitably by affliction, and affliction is the warp of human existence. Herbert wrote five poems called "Affliction," writing more poems under that title than any other—even love. The topic is, with him, almost an obsession, and he treats it in its subjective aspect as pain unbearable and inescapable: "My thoughts are all a case of knives" (*English Poems*, p. 328). In its salutary aspect he treats it as participatory in Jesus's afflictions and, potentially at least, capable of preparing sufferers for heaven: "Then shall those powers, which work for grief, / Enter thy pay, / And day by day, / Labour thy praise, and my relief, / With care and courage building me, / Till I reach heav'n, and much more thee" (*English Poems*, p. 328). But his focus is mostly on affliction as pain, and that is certainly brought to the fore in "Confession."

The pain of affliction is inescapable if we try to escape it. But perhaps it can be escaped if we don't. The last two stanzas of the poem turn to this:

> Onely an open breast
> Doth shut them [afflictions] out, so they cannot enter;
> Or, if they enter, cannot rest,
> But quickly seek some new adventure.
> Smooth open hearts no fastning have; but fiction
> Doth give a hold and handle to affliction.

Wherefore my faults and sinnes,
Lord, I acknowledge; take thy plagues away:
For since confession pardon winnes,
I challenge here the brightest day,
The clearest diamond: let them do their best,
They shall be thick and cloudie to my breast.
                    (Herbert, *English Poems*, p. 443)

Our finely wrought fictional efforts to construct hiding places from afflictions fail because, contrary to our expectations and desires, it's exactly the products of such efforts that give affliction purchase—"a hold and handle." Fictional complexities, the drama and fine language of the inner theater with all its twists and turns (Herbert uses the language of Chinese-box or Russian-doll joinery in the first three stanzas of the poem, but the point is the same), give afflictions something to latch on to. They make effigies that can be guyed (Herbert writes not long after Guy Fawkes), stuck with pins, tortured. The very detail and precision of the fictional confession, its artifice, increases affliction rather than reducing or minimizing it. Opposed to all that, to fiction in all its forms, are "smooth open hearts." They simply show themselves with clarity and spontaneity that outdoes the radiance of the "brightest day" or the "clearest diamond." Those need no effort to show themselves for what they are: they can at once be seen through, and there is nothing in them for affliction to fasten itself to. That is what the ideal confessor, and the ideal confession, should be like. A confession of that sort "pardon winnes" that nothing else can; affliction lodges on and in everything else.

Herbert, on this reading of the poem, is a lovely and energetic support for the view that fictionalized confessions, finely aware and richly responsible though they might be, aren't efficacious as confessions, for the reasons already given. The Russian dolls they make aren't us, and so in making them we don't show ourselves to the LORD but instead hide ourselves, all too often congratulating ourselves on the pleasing contours of our own depicted corruptions. Confessions like that don't "pardon winne" but instead provide just one more locus for affliction. Herbert is right about all this, and in being right he provides support and justification for the position here taken, which is that, as an obstacle-removing contrite and regretful avowal, the (cata)log is better than the novella.

But there are difficulties in Herbert's "Confession," and they're difficulties that may also afflict the position taken here. The troubling one is that what's advocated in the poem—the confession that is a transparent, frictionless, fictionless, self-showing—is advocated in a literary form and with a lexicon and syntax that are, in the terms of the poem itself, cunning: that is, highly wrought. If affliction's grief is a cunning guest, as Herbert says in the first two lines of the poem, then his poem, "Confession," is no less so. There's a sniff, and perhaps more than a sniff, of performative incoherence: what the poem performs is so deeply at odds with what it advocates that it's difficult to take its advocacy seriously.

There's an answer to that criticism, the strongest form of which observes that the poem isn't itself a confession. Rather, its topic is confession, and so there's no need for it to exemplify the virtues it recommends. What it does need to do is serve as a propaedeutic for the practice of confession, preferably in a self-removing or self-cancelling way, a way that shows its own uselessness as a confession. Artistry—fiction—may work very well as a way to remove wrong ideas about what it is to confess, so long as what the poem does, its own method, doesn't carry over or forward into the act of confessing itself. That's a good answer to the objection. But even it is called into question by other aspects of Herbert's work. For in that work there is at least one splendid example of a poem that portrays itself as a confession rather than, like "Confession," being about confession. I mean "Sinnes round," a poem in three six-line stanzas (*English Poems*, p. 430).

The poem has the LORD as its addressee ("Sorrie I am, my God, sorrie I am"), and it expresses sorrow for sin in thought, word, and deed, following the general confession of the Book of Common Prayer as Herbert would have known it. It takes, therefore, the form of a confession. It's a nonspecific one in that no particular sins are mentioned, with the possible exception of masturbation ("But words suffice not, where there are lewd intentions: / My hands do joyn to finish the inventions"). Herbert's attention, rather, is to the repetitive structure of sin: sinful thoughts lead to sinful words, and those lead to sinful deeds, which in turn lead again to sinful thoughts in an endless round. Sin is a circle, and so is the poem: the last line of each stanza is the first line of the next, and the last line of the last stanza is the first line of the first, which means that a recitation of the poem need never end—being, in that, just like sin's round, which is the poem's title. But this is a work of art: if not itself a Chinese box, then at least a highly wrought formal representation of its topic. It can hardly be understood as an instance of the kind of confession that "Confession" recommends, and the defense against the criticism that "Sinnes round" isn't itself a confession isn't so immediately available because the poem presents itself exactly as a confession to the LORD.

Pursuing that discussion leads deeper into exegesis of George Herbert, which isn't my topic here. I take both "Confession" and "Sinnes round" to show, with depth and beauty, something important about the kind of avowal that confession ought to be if it's to perform what it should, which is the removal of the obstacle of sin between the LORD and the confessor. To remove that obstacle, the confession ought to eschew, to the extent possible, the kinds of fiction that attend to the inner theater of motive, purpose, intention, and desire; it ought to attend, rather, to acts considered in their kinds, and it need avow them only as members of that kind, without avowing the details of their performance. In that way, no new obstacles between the sinner and the LORD are fabricated and the sinner's confession, like his gaze, is turned away from himself and toward the LORD, whence comes the only healing there is. The positive content of confession's avowals is, on this reading, almost (but not quite) irrelevant.

IN A LETTER WRITTEN IN 1629, RESPONDING TO A REQUEST FOR advice about confession, Angélique Arnauld (1591–1661), George Herbert's almost-exact contemporary, wrote this:

> Madame, I humbly ask you to have no anxiety concerning what you have to do [i.e., confess your sins] and to believe that you

need neither an examination of conscience nor any other preparation for it other than the real desire God has given you to live for him alone and to follow all the counsels that will be given to you so that you may follow this holy desire. This presupposes a true hatred of all that is opposed to God. You see that by a completely exceptional grace, he gives you every day greater light to follow him, leaving or embracing everything he shows you to oppose or to be necessary for the project he has shown you. A sick man who has an ardent desire to be healed has no difficulty in telling what is troubling him. His suffering makes him state his problem clearly and he easily explains his illness to the doctor. If you had spent an entire year examining your conscience with the most careful attentiveness, before God had touched your heart, you could not have been as prepared and, I would even say, you would not have known your faults as well as you do at the moment without any personal examination of conscience. It is grace alone that can give you such knowledge. (John J. Conley, *Adoration and Annihilation*, p. 72)

Arnauld was a Cistercian religious, professed in 1603 at the age of twelve without her full consent, and then re-professed in 1610 as an adult with enthusiasm. She was mostly thereafter resident at the Abbey of Port-Royal in Paris, of which she was for a time abbess; she was instrumental both in its reform in the first and second decade of the seventeenth century and in its close connection with the Jansenist movement and controversies of mid-century. Antoine Arnauld, one of the principal theologians of that movement, was her brother and she was closely acquainted with the Pascal siblings, Jacqueline and Blaise.

The extract quoted affirms, with brio, the position that introspection (examination of conscience) is both unnecessary as preparation for auricular confession and probably harmful. In order to make a good confession, you don't need to attend closely to your particular sins, and much less to their causes, the intentions that informed them, and their phenomenal feel. You are sick, Arnauld says to her correspondent; if you know that about yourself, and if you attend, with self-abnegation, to the LORD as healer, and if you avow your sickness and your need for graceful healing, you'll do everything necessary. You'll know what, thereafter, you need to do and, with sufficient grace, you'll be able to do it.

Arnauld doesn't, in the letter I've extracted, go into further detail about why the humble confession of sin-as-sickness is enough, and why examination of conscience is not needed. But the assumptions that inform such a position are clear enough. They accord with the discussion given above of the unreliability, superfluity, and egotism of confessions informed by close examination of conscience that tend, therefore, toward the Proustian in their depiction of the sinner's sins. What Arnauld wants is for the confessor to see her radical unworthiness before the LORD, and therefore to place herself under erasure. Confessors need to avow their nothingness; that avowal, that performance, is sufficient to remove the only obstacle there is or can be between the LORD and the confessor. Adoration of the LORD is tantamount to self-annihilation, and that is because adoration removes any sense of oneself as capable of existing without the LORD and thereby diverts one's attention from oneself and the particularity of one's sins toward the LORD. The direction of the gaze is changed, and it is that change which Mère Angélique presses upon her correspondent. A more distant assumption is that the gorgeous detail of our sense of ourselves as the center of the cosmos, our first-personal self-identifications as the experiencers of this or that, the performers of this or that, the rightful recipients of this or that, the athletically vicious or virtuous—all that is an artifact of the Fall, and bringing it to nothing is, in essence, what confession's avowal does. Arnauld and her school see this clearly.

AUGUSTINE'S AND HERBERT'S AND ARNAULD'S INTEREST IN contrite and regretful avowals has to do with making them to the LORD. Such avowals, however, can be made to other people, and an account of what they do—what the content of their performance is— when that's their audience must be in some respects different.

A good start can be made on this topic with Ludwig Wittgenstein. In 1936, when he was forty-seven, he wrote a confession. He sent the text to at least five people and, in December 1936 and January

1937, met face-to-face with some of them in Vienna and Cambridge to read them what he'd written and to elaborate upon it. He may also have made oral confession to people to whom he hadn't sent the written text, and it's clear from comments in letters to Wittgenstein that the written confession was passed on, with his permission, to people to whom he hadn't sent it directly. The text of the written confession isn't known to have survived, but we do have some accounts of one-on-one meetings at which he read it aloud; there are also some remarks about the written confession in letters by Wittgenstein. These materials aren't entirely in agreement with one another but they overlap sufficiently to make it clear that Wittgenstein had been, while in Norway in the autumn of 1936, considering the shape and the particulars of his life up to that time, had identified a number of things he'd done that weren't, as he saw it, as they should have been, and had written a document in which these misbehaviors were listed and in which he identified just what, as he saw it, was wrong with them. These things are what he confessed. He made regretful and fictive avowal, therefore, in writing and speech, of actions and intentions he wished otherwise, and in doing so he also made clear that he intended and hoped to avoid actions and intentions of those kinds in the future.

Wittgenstein took both the writing of the confession and the subsequent face-to-face oral confessions seriously. In November 1936, for instance, he wrote to G. E. Moore in the following way, anticipating a meeting at which his confession would be heard:

> Besides this all sorts of things have been happening inside me (I mean in my mind). I won't write about them now, but when I come to Cambridge as I intend to do for a few days about New Year, I hope to God I shall be able to talk to you about them; and I shall want your advice and your help in some very difficult and serious matters. (Brian McGuinness, ed., *Wittgenstein in Cambridge*, p. 257)

And it is clear that those who read and heard his confession understood that he took it seriously, even if they found it difficult to do so themselves. Fania Pascal, one of those to whom he sent the written confession and with whom he later met to read it, found the whole thing absurd in its solemnity and couldn't take it seriously. And even his sister Margaret, a recipient of at least the written confession, responds by writing to Ludwig that, "surely you know that I could counter every one of your confessed sins with the same or ones far worse in kind" (Brian McGuinness, ed. *Wittgenstein's Family Letters*, p. 211).

And indeed the sins, insofar as we can tell what they were, don't seem especially unusual or grave. Most of them involved, as Wittgenstein saw it, cowardice and/or deceit. He had, for example, collaborated with his brother Paul in misleading the authorities in Vienna about the degree of his Jewish ancestry—three of his grandparents were Jews, and in order to establish exemption from the Nuremberg race laws, the Wittgensteins claimed that only one was. And then he'd had a history of using corporal punishment on children when he'd been a schoolteacher in various Austrian villages in the 1920s, and in one case, in Otterthal in 1926 (Wittgenstein would have been thirty-six or thirty-seven), he'd hit an eleven-year-old boy hard enough to cause him to collapse, and perhaps to lose consciousness (the details remain unclear). A disciplinary hearing followed from this, and Wittgenstein confesses, according to one of the accounts, to having lied at that hearing. He seems to have been burdened by the lie much more than by the use of violence. That is probably because the use of violence by teachers upon children was as commonplace in the Austria of the 1920s as it had been in the Africa of the 360s (Augustine complains about it) and as it remained in the England of the 1960s, where it was dished out to me. Wittgenstein may also have confessed cowardice during his World War I military service, and he perhaps also confessed to having misled people about whether he'd ever had sex with anyone, but the accounts we have are vague and inconsistent on these last two points.

It's notable that Wittgenstein's written and oral confessions weren't, in these cases, made to those he'd offended. That's not to say he never did that. He did, for example, return to Otterthal in 1937 to make in-person apologies to some of the children he had offended (and who were no longer children, as the offences had been at least a decade earlier) and to their parents. He was, it seems, given a mixed reception, as is hardly surprising. But in the case under discussion here, he chooses as the recipients of his confession not those he's offended but, rather, those he knows well, his close friends and family—presumably, those who can hear him with a presupposition of intimacy and support. It's also notable that he both speaks and writes his confession. Neither form alone, it seems, would have sufficed for his purposes. In addition to writing his confession and sharing that written text with others, he wanted also to meet with at least some of them for oral confession. Why? He doesn't say, but it was clearly important to him: he went to a great deal of trouble, often against the inclinations of those he confessed to, to make those face-to-face meetings happened.

The triple structure of Wittgenstein's confessional act—first, thinking and writing in private; then sharing with others what had been written; then communicating what had been written orally and face-to-face—comports with, and illuminates, the structure of ordinary Christian practice. Considering your sins in camera, in the privacy of your bedchamber, doesn't suffice. If absolution is what's wanted, and Wittgenstein does seem to have wanted something like that, then there must be a public act. For Catholics, that's either a general oral confession made in the context of a communal liturgical celebration or a private oral confession of particular sins made before a priest. Only when the acts and intentions wished otherwise are given a form that permits them to be communicated to another or others can they be forgiven. Wittgenstein's written confession would have had fictive form—narrativized, highly interpreted, ornamented—as all such confessions do. This is confirmed by the tone of the surviving remarks about it by those to whom it was sent. They find it overwrought, both in the sense of being overexcited and in the sense of being overdramatized. Nietzsche, in writing about Augustine's *Confessions* to Franz Overbeck in 1885, captures the flavor of Fania Pascal's response to Wittgenstein's confession: "O this old rhetorician! How false and eye-rolling he is!" (James J. O'Donnell, *Confessions*, vol. 2, p. 227). Whether or not Wittgenstein's confession is overwrought, it is certainly wrought. All (written or spoken) confessions are, but it is especially not surprising to find this to be so in the case of one of the twentieth century's most thoroughly wrought writers. Wittgenstein is far, in his confessional practice, from Arnauld's rec- ommendation that examination of conscience ought to be eschewed and from Herbert's recommendation that fictionalized reminiscences are, because of their artistry, unlikely to do what confessions ought.

Wittgenstein's confessions, however, do show that, as in the Catholic rite of penance, the act of communicating your particular sins directly to another person, or feeling that you have done so, is important to the receiving of absolution. In the rite, it is the priest, acting as the LORD's representative and intermediary. Wittgenstein, having been baptized and confirmed as a Catholic, would have un- dergone the rite as a child. And while it isn't clear from what remains to us of what he wrote and said about his confession to what extent absolution is the right interpretive category for what he sought, it is clear that he wanted to change the course of his life by having and showing his contrition for his sins to others and by finding the pos- sibility thereby of living a life less marked by deceit and cowardice than the one he understands himself to have lived up to that point. Consider the following, from 1937:

> Last year with God's help I pulled myself together and made a confession. This brought me into more settled waters, into a better relation with people, and to a greater seriousness. But now it is as though I had spent all that, and I am not far from where I was before. I am cowardly beyond measure. If I do not correct this, I shall again drift entirely into those waters in which I was adrift then. (Ray Monk, *Duty of Genius*, p. 372)

The settled waters didn't last long for him, as they also don't for most Catholic participants in the rite of penance. But they were what he sought, and his identification of those settled waters with a combi- nation of better relations with others and greater seriousness about the shape of his own life makes good sense of his need to confess, in public and in private, and of the genre and meaning of his confession.

Wittgenstein's confession is, in essentials, a Catholic auricular confession lifted out of a sacramental context. It shows one aspect of what it means to confess to another person, rather than to the LORD. But it's also possible to confess, to regretfully and contritely avow what you take to be your offenses against another person exactly to that person. In such a case, further minor adjustments to the account are necessary. Those will be addressed in the discussion of penance, to come.

CHAPTER EIGHT

Penance

CONFESSION IS DIRECTED, FIRST AND LAST, TO THE LORD: IT's a contrite avowal that performs the turn of the gaze toward the LORD, who is the beautiful one, and away from sin, which is the ugliness of lack, the determination to embrace what is not. When you confess not to the LORD, nor to some third person not directly afflicted by your sin, but rather to someone you've directly damaged by your sin, confession becomes penance. Penance, like confession, is a performative avowal. But it is in one way more limited in scope than confesson (it's made directly to the sinned-against, while confession need not be) and in another way it is broader (it can, and typically does, involve more than the use of words).

A straightforward, if trivial, instance: You've broken a promise by which you were bound. Let's suppose it's a promise not to publish anything you've written without letting the editor of a particular journal have first refusal. You've had a long and mutually productive relationship with this editor, and you're more than acquaintances, perhaps almost friends. She, moreover, has been supportive of you and your work, publishing you when you badly needed to be published and providing, always, detailed and truthful commentary on your work. Nevertheless, you've broken your promise: seduced, perhaps, by money or the promise of greater fame, your latest and best piece is about to appear elsewhere, without your editor-friend's knowledge. You're troubled by your promise-breaking. You have lunch with her and confess. Not only that, you reaffirm your promise: in the future, you say, you intend to be bound by the *status quo ante*, and you're remorseful, contrite, and penitent for your offense. Your penance, you can see, requires more than simple apology. It also requires redress, and you tell her, with hesitation, that you've a suggestion about that: you've a piece that you've been working on for a while, now almost complete—you can email the almost-complete draft to her right now—and you'd like, if she finds it suitable, to publish it with her *gratis*. You'll renounce your usual fee. She accepts your apology, though not without expressing puzzlement and regret of her own for your sin—why didn't you tell her you were going to break your promise? She accepts, too, your suggestion for redress, and she says that she'll look at the piece as soon as you send it to her. She does, and a few months later it appears, *gratis* as you suggested.

What has happened here?

First, a breach between the sinner and the sinned-against editor has been contritely avowed. That avowal shows or, better, just is a turning of the sinner's gaze away from the sin and toward the one damaged by it. Your expression of contrition is that turning. You're looking now at the face of the one you've damaged, and your avowal is the verbal correlate of that look. When you do that before and to the LORD, the breach is at once healed because the LORD preveniently and always forgives and embraces: the LORD is love and that's how love works. When you do that before and to your sinned-against editor, matters are more complicated. She cannot, because she is herself damaged and sinful, receive your contrite gaze fully. She always, because she is herself damaged and sinful, looks away from it to some degree, and in looking away she opens again the breach you've brought into being. But she can, because she, like you, hasn't had the LORD's image and likeness completely erased by her sins, receive you and your contrite avowal to some degree, and the extent to which she does that is also the extent to which the division between you is removed.

Second, the closing of the breach, partial and incomplete though it is, suggests to you and to her that something further is appropriate. You've held out your hand to her in your confession and she has taken

it, which is a good thing and a necessary thing, but that good and necessary thing suggests something more. She is still bleeding, you can
see, and you want to salve her wounds. The balm is the offer of a new
piece, a real sample of the work of your hands, for nothing, which is
to say for love. Her acceptance of that balm makes it efficacious. Had
you not offered the balm (performed your penance) and had she not
received it as an offering, something would have been left undone:
confession's avowal goes only so far. Such avowals move those who
make them and those who receive them toward further actions in
rather the same way that a kiss offered and received leads, as naturally
as an emerald is green, to further exchange.

One interpretation of this case is in terms of contract and debt:
you've broken your contract—your original promise—with her, and
now you're discharging your debt. Her receipt of your penance—the
gratis publication—clears the account, and you can now proceed as
you were. But this is not the best way to see it. A better way to see it,
more in accord with the thought that our good actions participate in
the LORD's (a thought that Christians can't do without), is to see
your confession as a gift, her receipt of it as gratitude for that gift, and
your consequent penance as further, reciprocal gratitude for your
gift's having been received as such. The economy in play is one of gift
and gratitude rather than one of contract and obligation. You don't
owe one another anything; you can give one another gifts; and when
gifts are received as gifts, which is to say with gratitude, then further
gifting and receiving follows, as the sun shines when the clouds part.
Effort enters when a gift is refused, or when it is received as discharge
of a debt. That effort twists the economy of gift into that of contract
and thereby distances it from the economy that relates us to the
LORD. Without that effort, always a work of sin, the gift remains a
gift, and it prompts always the Eucharistic thank-you. Your penance,
consequent upon your confessional avowal, is what follows from that
avowal when you're moving, like a fish in the sea, within the economy
of gift. It's what you do. Not to do it, to refuse the penance, would be
to take yourself out of that ocean and to flop about, exhaustedly, back
in the realm of contract and obligation. Penance, on this reading, is no
burden and no obligation but rather the outflow of a prevenient gift.

That's why the Catholic archive typically says that the extent to which penance is refused is the extent to which forgiveness isn't received: the evidence of your having received the gift is exactly that you do what gratitude suggests, and that is what penance is.

Of course, it needs emphasizing again, the gift economy is never fully present in human relations. You and your editor can't, and therefore don't, offer one another pure gifts; you can't, and therefore don't, take yourselves quite out of the economy of debt and obligation. Your penance will inevitably seem, to you and to her, in part discharge of an obligation that brings new obligations with it and to that extent a burden rather than a gift. We are not, that's to say, the LORD. But thinking about the LORD — that is, doing theology — helps us to see what we are and wherein our damage consists.

There's a third thing that's happened in this example, in addition to the turning of the gaze avowed in confession and the breach healing brought about by the offer and receipt of the gift of penance. It's the transfiguration of the past. In the past, you broke a promise by offering to another outlet a piece of your work reserved for your editor and her journal. You came to see that act as regrettable. You wished it otherwise, and you were remorseful and contrite for it; you avowed your contrition and did penance. The act remains, however, just what it was, or so it may seem: you have in fact broken your promise, and your promise has, therefore, been broken. That state of affairs remains, like all states of affairs in the past, just what it was, no matter what you later come to say and think and do about it. Time has moved on, and moved you on with it, and what you did is now inaccessible to you. So, again, it may seem.

But recall, as already shown, that Christian thought and practice don't, as a matter of principle, permit the past to be inaccessible in that way. Time's passage doesn't work like that. The linear model, commonsensical though it may seem, is incorrect. The liturgy in general and the sacraments in particular show time to be fully legible only when measured by repeated cycles rather than by a single line. Time's passage is like the inbreath followed by the outbreath or the systolic contraction and diastolic relaxation of the heart muscle: a rhythmic repeater, world without end. Death is a complete explanation for the coming to an end of the cycles of the breath and of the heart. In the absence of death, a state that the liturgy shows and anticipates and that will be fully evident in the resurrection, those cycles do not end. Instead, in their endless repetition, they provide life.

Among the features of real time (that is, liturgical time) is that it makes present again and again (as the timeline would have it) events that belong to the past (again, as the timeline would have it). It doesn't do so solely, or even principally, by way of commemoration. No, the flesh and blood of Jesus, to take the paradigmatic instance, are really present everywhere the Eucharist is celebrated. Space-time—recall that temporal and spatial extension are coordinate, which explains that locution—is folded upon and around Jesus's flesh and blood and, therefore, also upon and around the events of that flesh, its birth, death, resurrection, and ascension. The flesh that undergoes, in the atemporal present, those things is also, without reservation or remainder, the flesh on your tongue when you receive the Eucharist. That infolding of time around Jesus is what makes possible the real presence of other, indeed of all, past-according-to-the-timeline events in the apparent present.

This understanding of things has immediate application to the possibility of transfiguring—making really different—contritely avowed past states of affairs for which penance is done. When they are contritely avowed before the LORD, identified as states of affairs the confessor wishes otherwise, they are brought to Jesus, who is really present where and when the confession is made. To say that Jesus is really present there is also to say that the three persons of the Trinity are really present there; good Trinitarian theology requires that to be said (when we're doing Trinitarian theology, that is, which isn't, thankfully, all the time), and I'll indicate their presence and Jesus's presence when confession is made simply by saying that the LORD, the one who is, is present.

All past events and states of affairs—your promise-breaking, Napoleon's retreat from Moscow, the shape of Cleopatra's nose, Aśoka's embrace of Buddhism, Pol Pot's genocidal revolution—are present, atemporally, to the LORD, whether they're in the past or the present or the future from the viewpoint of those, like us, subject to linear, death-dealing time here in the devastation. That presence is true not only of your promise-breaking but also of that promise-breaking contritely avowed before the LORD and to your sinned-against editor, as well as of that promise-breaking penitentially acted upon as you make redress to her. What was once, according to the timeline, just an act of promise-breaking, unregretted, is now, temporally speaking, something different. It has been transfigured by being forgiven, and it is thereby taken up into the divine economy of gift. It has, like the wounds on Jesus's flesh or those on the flesh of the martyrs, been changed from a bleeding, open wound into a smooth, white cicatrix. Promise-breaking unrepented, unregretted, unconfessed is really different, different in the order of being, from promise-breaking repented, regretted, confessed. It isn't that your actions change it. That isn't within the power of creatures. It's rather that your actions, the actions that begin from wishing your promise-breaking otherwise, remove from that (past) action what makes it a sin, which is the turning away from the LORD in it. What makes promise-breaking a sin is what it shares with all sins: a pure negative, a grasp after nothing. A sin is a hole or rent or tear in the fabric of graceful gift that is the cosmos, including ourselves; the LORD is always-atemporally-preveniently eager to mend the tear—needle and thread at the ready, as it were. All we have to do—recall Angélique Arnauld's emphasis on the love of the LORD and the concomitant annihilation of oneself before the LORD as the only necessities, introspection be damned—is look at and to the LORD, and the tear is healed, with elegant stitchery. The rent was made and it was healed; cloth torn and stitched looks different from cloth never torn, and the difference, once again, is the cicatrix. But you don't have to mend the rent yourself; you don't even have to provide the correct account of what made it, how large it is, or what you had to do with making it; all you have to do is turn to the LORD with the sincerely contrite thought, "I would it were otherwise," and it is.

It's important to distinguish the view expressed in the preceding paragraph from one that overlaps with it and may be hard to distinguish from it. The obvious difference between an unregretted sin and a regretted one is, for everyone I suppose, that the one is unregretted and the other regretted. One way of construing that difference is to say that regretted sins have their place in the life of the one who regrets them, a place that is changed, transfigured even, by the act of regretting them. That's true, so far as it goes. A sin you don't wish otherwise, whether because you don't see it as a sin or because you do and nevertheless glory in it, has a different place in your life than one you both see as sinful and regret as such. That kind of transfiguration has its importance. It's real. But the view set out here claims more: that the damage caused by past sins can be transfigured (not erased) for the cosmos as well as for the sinner. Penance, as the outflow of contrite avowal and the acknowledgment of the prevenient gift of the healing of sin's damage, transforms, in the order of being, the bleeding wounds the cosmos bears into its scars.

BUT AREN'T THERE MANY SINS FOR WHICH NO PENANCE IS possible? If so, doesn't that mean some sins can't be healed? It seems, for instance, that some sins aren't directed at anyone in particular, or even at any group in particular, but are, rather, sins of participation in some sinful order of things. In such cases, it's not clear to whom contrite avowals should be made, and much less what redress penance might offer. And even when there is a particular sinned-against entity, whether person or group, it might be that they're dead, otherwise unavailable, or unwilling to accept confessions or penances. In such cases, it isn't clear what confession or penance might consist of or how they could properly be done.

It's true that there are sins in all these categories. In the example just discussed, your editor might, on learning that you'd broken your promise, choose to have nothing more to do with you. In that case, you could neither offer penance nor have any penance accepted. And, to take an instance discussed earlier, if you're contrite for species-extinctions, and for the last dinosaur's last sigh in particular, it's certainly the case that no living dinosaur can receive (or reject) your avowals or your penance. And of course there are sins directed at no one in particular, sins, too, that are unavoidable while life continues. But in none of these categories is it impossible to cultivate regret, contrition, and confession, or to perform penance.

Suppose, to take the simplest case, that your editor had indeed refused your apology and your penance. Perhaps she'd discovered your promise-breaking independently of you, and she will, because of that discovery, have nothing more to do with you. That would rule out your apology to her and your offer of redress. But you can still confess to the LORD, and from that avowal and the assurance of forgiveness it receives, other penances may flow. A good confessor would encourage you to see what they might be. Most generally, they'll be free gifts of whatever it's possible for you, in your situation and with your talents and capacities, to give. Recall that acts of penance aren't repayments. They don't belong to the economy of obligation. Rather, they're acts that someone grateful for forgiveness naturally does. They're a participation in the excess of the LORD's gifts, and so they will, to the limited extent possible for you, show that excess to others. If those you've sinned against can't or won't receive your gifts to them, your sins are still transfigured by the LORD. There'll always be plenty that remains untransfigured. The world won't, until the end of all things, be short of bleeding wounds not yet scarred over, and some among those will be wounds produced by the incapacity of those damaged by the sins of others to receive confession and penance from those others. You can lament those wounds. But that is all.

More interesting, and certainly more complex, are participations in complex structures that entail damage, even damage on a massive scale. I am, for example, a citizen of and taxpayer in a large, late-capitalist sovereign state. It follows at once that I am also, and unavoidably, a participant in large-scale systemic violence; in modes of production and consumption that contribute to the degradation of the global ecosystem, with all the epiphenomena of that degradation, including current equivalents of the last dinosaur's last sigh; and in modes of production and consumption that have among their necessary conditions sweatshop labor, wage slavery, and the existence of a very large gap between the conditions under which the poorest subsist on our planet and those within which the rich disport themselves. I live in the United States, whose GDP per citizen is more than two hundred times that of any of the half-dozen states lowest on that list.

The disparity is even greater if the state highest on that list (Monaco) is compared with the lowest (Burundi—these are 2015 rankings): in that comparison, the multiplier is approximately six hundred. These kinds of facts can properly be lamented; I can, and sometimes I do, feel contrition for my part in them, and for the fact of them—for, most broadly, the fact that this is how we humans have organized our life together. But I cannot extract myself from these arrangements—from the extraterritorial killing of civilians with drones by the military forces of my state, from the wastage of food in my immediate locale while malnutrition and starvation are common elsewhere, and so on. These arrangements approach death in their unavoidability. They provide the fabric of my existence. Nothing I can do will heal them. The wounds bleed, so profusely that no one can stanch them. Like death, these wounds won't be cicatrized until the end of all things. That things are as they are in these respects is the most glaring, systemic, and largely unalterable effect of the Fall.

I would that these things were otherwise. I expect that you feel the same way. Contrition for them is appropriate and sometimes possible. Avowal of them, in the form of confession, can also be done, though it is difficult because of the complexity of the political and economic arrangements that produce these effects. What, exactly, should be acknowledged? Minimally, that violent death, death by starvation and avoidable disease, avoidable suffering in mind and body, and luxurious living predicated upon the poverty and suffering of others, are deplorable evidences of the Fall. But decisions as to what constitutes luxurious living, which sufferings are avoidable, and when lethal violence is defensible—those are difficult matters whose very difficulty provides one more state of affairs to be wished otherwise. I take no position on the substance of them here, other than to note that penance for these deplorabilities is in small ways possible. The degree of your awareness of these states of affairs, and your location within them, will suggest to you modes of living that contribute, however insignificantly, to their redress, as well as suggesting to you modes of living that deepen the damage we find all around us.

It's one of the gifts and blessings of the Christian archive (and not only of it but it's the one from within which I write) that from its beginning until now it has worked to discriminate what in the devastated world is to be deplored from what is to be celebrated and to form Christians in awareness of these differences and thereby to help us (that is, we Christians) to see what lament and contrition should be directed toward. Augustine provides a version of this discrimination in his treatise *De civitate dei* (The City of God), composed during the early decades of the fifth century: he acknowledges that the two cities, that of death which serves the world and that of life which serves the LORD, are inextricably linked in history and that we are not good at discriminating who belongs to which city. He nevertheless thinks it easy enough in principle to discern the difference between the two cities and the characteristic marks of the conduct proper to each. Among the fundamental differences between the two, he writes, is that the inhabitants of the LORD's city learn, over time and always imperfectly, to lament their implication in and inextricability from the violence that marks the human city, while those formed exclusively, or almost so, by and for the human city do not see that such violence needs lamenting. Augustine likes, using the words of Psalm 24 (in the version known to him), to implore the LORD to deliver him from his necessities (*de necessitatibus meis erue me*). Such a demand is a form of lament and contrition and confession, laced with hope and realistic in the knowledge that such delivery won't come until the end. Imploring the LORD in this way is incumbent upon all Christians.

THE OTHERWISE-ATTITUDES, WITH PENANCE AS THEIR CULMInation, lament as their entry point, remorse as their deformed sibling, contrition as their heart, and avowal as the beginning of the transfiguration of what's regretted, lie close to the heart of the Christian life. They're given liturgical form in the sacrament of penance, but they have a much broader part to play in the Christian life than that. Their cultivation and formation is an essential element in the love of the LORD and in the recognition of the difference between the LORD and us. Someone who has no regrets is someone not fully human and certainly someone not much formed as a Christian.

Self-deceit can, of course, be practiced. There are people, and perhaps you are one, who say that the world as they find it is, to them, entirely satisfactory. There's nothing in it they wish otherwise, they say and think. If that's your case, you are a complacent fool; a cure for your foolishness might be attempted by repeated visits to and extended contemplations of abattoirs, deathbeds, torture chambers, concentration camps, places where abortions are performed, and locations where devastations have been produced by fire and flood. If those don't work—if, on seeing them, you embrace them as just how things should be—then you are beyond argument and will find correction when the pain of your own life yields, for you, the hope that it might be otherwise and in that way rebuts your optimism (which, eventually, in one way or another, it will). Even Gautama Śākyamuni, as the story goes, though sheltered by riches and protective parents from any knowledge of suffering and old age and death, did eventually come to see and know these things, and when he did he was moved by the sense that this is not how things ought to be and that a remedy for them must be found.

There are others, more subtle and thoughtful, and far from foolish, who acknowledge that the world doesn't seem, to most of us most of the time, satisfactory and that for most of us, including themselves, there are elements or aspects of it ordinarily wished otherwise. But, they say, they've learned better, or they are at least on the way to learning better; they've adjusted themselves to the world as they find it, have permitted themselves to be disciplined by it, and have learned that preferring things otherwise when they cannot, it seems, be otherwise is a waste of time and energy. (Different things would have to be said about states of affairs that can be made otherwise: Seneca's suicide is prompted by something inevitable, as it seems to him, something incapable of change—namely, disgrace and an emperor's anger. Suicide wouldn't, even for a high-octane Stoic, be an appropriate response to easily remedied hunger—why kill yourself when there's a grape to hand for peeling?) Such wishes ought, they think, to be reduced as closely as possible to zero; life will then be calm, acceptance of its vagaries will be possible, and the futility and childishness of raging against them may be transformed into mature acceptance. They have, perhaps, adopted the practices and attitudes of some kinds of Stoicism and Buddhism (there are similar strands in some versions of Christianity, too), methods that attempt the discrimination of what cannot be controlled or altered from what can, and methods that move toward eliminating otherwise-wishes directed toward the former. Like Edith Piaf, they hope to be able to say that they have no regrets, or at least that they have no regrets for what isn't susceptible to change—which includes the past in its entirety. Death is the test case here: if its inevitability is accepted, then it won't, on this view, be lamented or regretted or wished otherwise.

This is a defensible view or, better, family of views, even if it is not a true one. But its defensibility depends upon the thought that there are states of affairs that can't be transfigured by preferring them otherwise, and I've shown, in the course of this book, why that assumption doesn't and can't belong to the grammar of Christianity. To be Christian involves the view that the past is also present and that it can be transfigured. It involves, as well, the thought that even death will at last be transfigured. Otherwise-attitudes, then, for Christians, are essential, and they are also widespread, and properly so, among pagans. If there are human creatures completely without them, they are vanishingly rare and of interest principally for clinical reasons. The otherwise-attitudes may, though with difficulty, be disciplined toward removal: you may, for instance, learn to say, when hearing of the death of your child, that you already knew you'd begotten a mortal and so you are not moved, you regret neither having begotten your child nor the fact that they've died. But it's difficult to undertake and maintain such discipline, and doing so involves commitment to assumptions about one's capacity to accurately tell the difference between what's inevitable and what's not, whose truth is far from obvious.

But this is not to say that regret and its kin are an unmixed good in human, or Christian, life. The otherwise-attitudes can, like all goods, be malformed, and a good traditional label for their most characteristic deformity is scrupulosity. Scrupulosity, in its extreme forms, is life's collapse under the burden of an overdeveloped awareness of sin and damage. Death is everywhere, it's true; no action that we humans can undertake is free from ambiguity and implication in sin, it's true; our own particular sins are, it seems, ineradicable, it's true. And so on. Just as lament's characteristic deformity is despair, so the deformity proper to all the otherwise-attitudes, and especially evident in remorse in its extreme forms, is a scrupulosity that deletes joy and deletes, too, the possibility of participation in the sacramental life. The pious Catholic so burdened by his sin that he is unable to confess it because he cannot avow perfect contrition is a stock figure in Catholic literature. He, like those who find nothing in the world or themselves to regret, is a fool. If the cure for those who find nothing to regret is close contemplation of the world's horrors and their own contribution to them, his cure is close contemplation of the traces of glory in the world and of his own participation in and contribution to them. Such traces are everywhere, and they are to be celebrated. Those traces are signalled always in the texture of the sacramental life, the very existence of which is among them, and the cultivation of the otherwise-attitudes is, though essential, in the end a subaltern part of the Christian life, as is evident in the fact that the sacrament of penance transmutes those regrets and laments and contritions into the certainty of forgiveness. A life lived without regret, outside the otherwise-attitudes, is less than Christian and less than human. But a life lived without hope, outside the glory of the gift, is altogether un-Christian and, in the end, not possible.

Purgatory is the best Christian word for the counterfactual life—that is, for the life ordered in significant part by wishing the world and oneself otherwise. Mostly, for Catholic Christians and some others, purgatory has been understood as a postmortem condition, in which suffering purifies those undergoing it so that they may be ready for the intimacy with the LORD that will be found in heaven. Being in purgatory, on this understanding, is a condition with only one end, which is salvation. But the idea of purgatory can easily be extended into this life, and for advocates of universalism, among whom I count myself, so doing is an obvious move. If that move is made, then all the sin and damage and suffering of this life becomes possibly purgatorial: it leaves open a response to damage that moves those who make it, whether they know it or not, eventually toward the LORD. Dying still damaged, still unready, still shrouded by sin and damage unregretted, uncontritioned, unconfessed, and unpenanced (and which among us won't do that?) will guarantee further counterfactualism after death—the ordinary, Dantesque, understanding of purgatory.

But understanding the counterfactual life here below, in the devastation, as itself and already purgatorial permits what all Christians should want, which is a leavening of their regrets, which should be many and deep and agonizing ("A Presence of Departed Acts— /At window—and at Door," as Emily Dickinson puts it), with the certain knowledge that those regrets are already received and already transfigured.

BIBLIOGRAPHY

I'm grateful to those, living and dead, who composed the works listed below. No one can think without provocation, and these have been my principal provocateurs on the topics of this book. The following list contains works I found stimulating while writing this book, as well as all those mentioned or quoted in the body of the book.

Aciman, André. *The Enigma Variations.* New York: Farrar, Straus and Giroux, 2017.

Aquinas, Thomas. *Summa Contra Gentiles.* Rome: Leonine Commission, 1934.

Augustine. *Confessions.* Edited and translated by Carolyn J.-B. Hammond. 2 vols. Cambridge, MA: Harvard University Press, 2014, 2016.

———. *De civitate Dei.* Edited by Bernard Dombart and Alphonse Kalb. 2 vols. Darmstadt: Wissenschaftliche Buchgesellschaft, 1981.

Austen, Jane. *Emma.* Edited by Fiona Stafford. New York: Penguin Random House, 1996.

Baumann, Peter, and Monika Betzler, ed. *Practical Conflicts: New Philosophical Essays.* Cambridge, UK: Cambridge University Press, 2004.

Beale, Jonathan. "Wittgenstein's Confession." *New York Times*, September 18, 2018. https://www.nytimes.com/2018/09/18/opinion/wittgensteins-confession-philosophy.html.

Cates, Diana Fritz. *Aquinas on the Emotions: A Religious-Ethical Inquiry.* Washington, DC: Georgetown University Press, 2009.

Celan, Paul. *Poems of Paul Celan.* Translated by Michael Hamburger. New York: Persea Books, 1988.

———. *Schneepart.* Tübingen: Suhrkamp, 2002.

Conley, John J. *Adoration and Annihilation: The Convent Philosophy of Port-Royal.* Notre Dame, IN: University of Notre Dame Press, 2009.

Dickinson, Emily. *The Poems of Emily Dickinson: Reading Edition.* Edited by Ralph W. Franklin. Cambridge, MA: Belknap Press, 1998.

Fish, Stanley. *The Living Temple: George Herbert and Catechizing.* Berkeley, CA: University of California Press, 1978.

———. *Self-Consuming Artifacts: The Experience of Seventeenth-Century Literature.* Berkeley, CA: University of California Press, 1972.

Frost, Robert. *Collected Poems, Prose, & Plays.* New York: Library of America, 1995.

Gaita, Raimond. *Good and Evil: An Absolute Conception.* 2nd ed. New York: Routledge, 2004.

Griffiths, Paul J. *Christian Flesh.* Stanford, CA: Stanford University Press, 2018.

———. *Decreation: The Last Things of All Creatures.* Waco, TX: Baylor University Press, 2014.

———. *Intellectual Appetite: A Theological Grammar.* Washington, DC: Catholic University of America Press, 2009.

———. *Song of Songs.* Grand Rapids, MI: Brazos Press, 2011.

———. "Which Are the Words of Scripture?" *Theological Studies* 72, no. 4 (2011): 703–22.

Herbert, George. *The English Poems of George Herbert.* Edited by Helen Wilcox. Cambridge, UK: Cambridge University Press, 2007.

Hirshfield, Jane. *The October Palace.* San Francisco: Harper, 1994.

Hopkins, Gerard Manley. *The Collected Works of Gerard Manley Hopkins.* Vol. 2, *Correspondence 1882–1889*, edited by R. K. R. Thornton and Catherine Phillips. Oxford: Oxford University Press, 2013.

———. *Selected Poetry.* Edited by Catherine Phillips. Oxford: Oxford University Press, 1998.

James, Henry. *Complete Stories, 1898–1910.* Edited by Denis Donoghue. New York: Library of America, 1996.

Kahn, Leonard. "Conflict, Regret, and Modern Moral Philosophy." In *New Waves in Ethics*, edited by Thom Brooks, 7–27. London: Palgrave Macmillan, 2011.

Kedia, Gayannée, and Hilton, Denis J. "Hot As Hell! The Self-Conscious Nature of Action Regrets." *Journal of Experimental Social Psychology* 47 (2011): 490–93.

Kempowski, Walter. *All For Nothing.* Translated by Anthea Bell. New York: New York Review Books, 2018.

Kolnai, Aurel. "Forgiveness." *Proceedings of the Aristotelian Society* 74 (1973–1974): 91–106.

Krasznahorkai, László. *Baron Wenckheim's Homecoming.* Translated by Ottilie Mulzet. New York: New Directions, 2019.

———. *Satantango*. Translated by George Szirtes. New York: New Directions, 2013.

Landman, Janet. *Regret: The Persistence of the Possible*. New York: Oxford University Press, 1993.

Leopardi, Giacomo. *Passions*. Translated by Tim Parks. New Haven and London: Yale University Press, 2014.

———. *Zibaldone*. Edited by Michael Caesar and Franco D'Intino. Translated by Kathleen Baldwin, Richard Dixon, David Gibbons, Ann Goldstein, Gerard Slowey, Martin Thom, and Pamela Williams. New York: Farrar, Straus and Giroux, 2013.

Lombardo, Nicholas E. *The Logic of Desire: Aquinas on Emotion*. Washington, DC: Catholic University of America Press, 2010.

McBride, Eimar. *Strange Hotel*. London: Faber and Faber, 2020.

McGuinness, Brian, ed. *Wittgenstein in Cambridge: Letters and Documents 1911–1951*. 4th ed. Malden, MA: Blackwell, 2008.

———, ed. *Wittgenstein's Family Letters: Corresponding with Ludwig*. Translated by Peter Winslow. London and New York: Bloomsbury Academic, 2019.

Miner, Robert. *Aquinas on the Passions: A Study of Summa Theologiae, 1a2ae 22-48*. Cambridge, UK: Cambridge University Press, 2011.

Monk, Ray. *Ludwig Wittgenstein: The Duty of Genius*. New York: Free Press, 1990.

Murnane, Gerald. *The Plains*. London: Text Publishing, 2017.

Oakes, Edward T. "Ludwig Wittgenstein Confesses." *First Things*, June 1992. https://www.firstthings.com/article/1992/06/ludwig-wittgenstein-confesses.

O'Donnell, James J., ed. *Augustine: Confessions*. 3 vols. Oxford: Clarendon Press, 1992.

Olick, Jeffrey K. *The Politics of Regret: On Collective Memory and Historical Responsibility*. New York: Routledge, 2007.

Pascal, Blaise. "Écrit sur la conversion du pécheur." In *Pascal: Oeuvres complètes*, 2 vols., edited by Michel le Guern, 2:99–102. Paris: Éditions Gallimard, 1998, 2000.

———. "Prière pour demander à Dieu le bon usage des maladies." In *Pascal: Oeuvres complètes*, 2 vols., edited by Michel le Guern, 2:183–93. Paris: Éditions Gallimard, 1998, 2000.

Phillips, Adam. *Missing Out: In Praise of the Unlived Life*. New York: Farrar, Straus and Giroux, 2013.

Proeve, Michael, and Steven Tudor. *Remorse: Psychological and Jurisprudential Perspectives*. New York: Routledge, 2010.

Roberts, Robert C. *Spiritual Emotions: A Psychology of Christian Virtues*. Grand Rapids, MI: Eerdmans, 2007.

Rorty, Amélie O. "Agent Regret." In *Explaining Emotions*, edited by Amélie O. Rorty, 489–506. Berkeley, CA: University of California Press, 1980.

Saffrey, Colleen, Amy Summerville, and Neal J. Roese. "Praise for Regret: People Value Regret Above Other Negative Emotions." *Motivation and Emotion* 32, no. 1 (2008): 46–54.

Scheler, Max. *The Nature of Sympathy*. New Brunswick, NJ: Transaction Publishers, 2008.

———. "Repentance and Rebirth." In *On the Eternal in Man*, 35–59. New Brunswick, NJ: Transaction Publishers, 2010.

Schmitz, Kenneth L. *The Gift: Creation*. Milwaukee, WI: Marquette University Press, 1982.

Smith, Nick. *I Was Wrong: The Meanings of Apologies*. Cambridge, UK: Cambridge University Press, 2008.

Solomon, Robert C. *The Passions: Emotions and the Meaning of Life*. 2nd ed. Indianapolis, IN: Hackett, 1993.

———. *True to Our Feelings: What Our Emotions Are Telling Us*. New York: Oxford University Press, 2006.

Stein, Edith. *Zum Problem der Einfühlung*. Freiburg: Herder & Herder, 2008.

Tanner, Kathryn. *God and Creation in Christian Theology: Tyranny or Empowerment?* Minneapolis, MN: Fortress, 1988.

Tessman, Lisa. *Burdened Virtues: Virtue Ethics for Liberatory Struggles*. New York: Oxford University Press, 2005.

Tranströmer, Tomas. *Bright Scythe*. Translated by Patty Crane. Louisville, KY: Sarabande Books, 2015.

Tudor, Steven. *Compassion and Remorse: Acknowledging the Suffering of Others*. Leuven: Peeters, 2001.

Williams, Bernard. *Moral Luck*. Cambridge, UK: Cambridge University Press, 1982.

———. *Problems of the Self*. Cambridge, UK: Cambridge University Press, 1976.

Winner, Lauren F. *The Dangers of Christian Practice: On Wayward Gifts, Characteristic Damage, and Sin*. New Haven, NJ: Yale University Press, 2018.

Zeelenberg, Marcel. "The Use of Crying Over Spilled Milk: A Note on the Rationality and Functionality of Regret." *Philosophical Psychology* 12, no. 3 (1999): 325–40.

INDEX

PAUL J. GRIFFITHS formerly held the Warren Chair of Catholic Theology at Duke Divinity School. He is the author of numerous books, including *Christian Flesh* and *The Practice of Catholic Theology: A Modest Proposal.*

CPSIA information can be obtained
at www.ICGtesting.com
Printed in the USA
LVHW081430150121
676564LV00015B/458